Australia

Series editor Lesley Firth
Edited by Julia Kirk
Design Robert Wheeler
Picture Research Elizabeth Ogilvie
Production Rosemary Bishop
Consultant Alan Shearman
Illustrations Alex Gencur
              Ron Hayward Associates
              Tony Payne
              John Shackell
Maps Matthews & Taylor Associates

First published 1977
Macdonald Educational Ltd.
Holywell House, Worship Street
London EC2A 2EN

© Macdonald Educational
Limited 1977

ISBN 0 382-06183 7

Published in the United
States by Silver Burdett
Company, Morristown, N.J.
1978 Printing

Library of Congress
Catalog Card No. 78-56598

Photographic sources Key to
positions of illustrations: *(T)* top, *(C)*
centre, *(B)* bottom, *(L)* left, *(R)* right,
(M) middle.
Australian News and Information Service
*13, 15(BR), 18(TL), 19(BL,BR),
20(TL,BR), 21(TR,BR), 22(TL,BR),
23(TR), 25(TR), 28(BR), 30(BR),
32(M), 36(B), 40(BL,BR), 41(T),
43(T), 44(T), 47(BL), 49(TL,TR,BL),
50(BR), 51(BL), 52(B).* BBC *31(TL).*
Jonathan Cape *31(BL).* J. Allan Cash
14(TL),15(TR), 41(BR). Cinema
Bookshop *12(BR).* Colorpix *16(TL),
34(BR), 35(T).* Colour Library
International *9(TR), 29(TL,TR),
39(TR), 42(BL).* Gerry Cranham
42(TR). Mary Evans *33(BR), 34(TL).*
GTO Films *31(BR).* Robert Harding
18(BR), 46(TR), 53(TR). Historical
Picture Service *11(T), 32(BL), 35(BL,
BR), 37(BR).* Rob MacIntyre *23(BR),
27(TR).* MacQuitty Collection *24(TL).*
Mansell Collection *36(T), 37(TL).*
Picturepoint *9(BL), 10(BL), 19(TL),
28(TR), 29(BL), 30(T), 38(BR),
45(TL), 47(BR), 51(T).* Qantas
Airlines *46(TL).* Radio Times Hulton
Picture Library *34(BL), 37(TR,BL).*
G. R. Roberts *11(M), 14(B), 21(T,BL),
33(BL), 39(TL), 41(BL), 44(BL),
45(BL), 46(M,BR), 47(T).* Royal
Aeronautical Society *49(BR).* Spectrum

19(TR). Sydney Bulletin *50(TR),
53(BL,M).* Syndication International
40(TL), 42(TL). Tate Gallery *31(TR),
33(T).* Neil Williams *11(BL,BR),
16(BR), 17(TR), 23(TL), 24(TR,M,
BR), 25(TL), 26(TL), 27(TL), 52(TR),
53(BR).* Zefa *8(TL,BL,BR), 10(BR),
12(TR), 32(T), 38(TL,TR), 45(TR),
48(T), 50(TL).*

Endpaper: the magnificent Sydney Opera
House situated on Bennelong Point, with
Sydney Harbour Bridge in the background.
Opened in 1973 and designed by the Danish
architect, Joern Utzon, the Opera House is
a centre for international arts, including
opera, ballet and orchestral concerts.

Page 6: a view from the top of Ayers Rock,
towards the Simpson Desert in Northern
Territory. This huge rock in the Central
Desert was formed in the ice age. Its
beautiful colour changes at dawn and dusk
are famous throughout Australia.

Australia

the land and its people

Elizabeth Cornelia

Macdonald Educational

Contents

A continent of contrasts

A wide, brown land

Australia is an island continent of 7,682,300 square kilometres and the sixth largest country in the world.

It is a country of contradictions: one of the most sparsely populated countries yet one of the most urbanized; the smallest and most arid continent, yet one of the most prosperous nations; among the oldest land masses on earth, yet one of the last to be developed. One third of Australia lies within the tropics, while huge tracts of alpine country in the south-east, covered in snow in winter, support thriving ski resorts.

Australia is the only continent occupied by a single nation, whose people maintain a Western European lifestyle in the midst of their South East Asian neighbours. Perhaps the greatest contrast is between the outback of vast, flat deserts with few people and the urban sprawl of the coastal cities where most Australians live and work.

Water is a major problem. Australia has the lowest average annual rainfall of all the continents and one of the highest evaporation rates. About one third of the country is desert.

Natural beauty

Australia has many striking physical features which are among the world's natural wonders. Ayers Rock in the Central Desert, famous for its beautiful colour changes from sunrise to sunset, is the world's largest rock, rising 335 metres above a sand and gravel plain. The Great Barrier Reef, a coral reef extending 2000 kilometres along the North Queensland coast, is dotted with coral islands and supports abundant marine life.

The tropical rainforests of North Queensland are in great contrast to the vast, flat desert of the Nullarbor Plain in South and Western Australia. The Nullarbor, true to its name, has no trees, but it does have the longest straight train line in the world running across its endless emptiness.

Lake Eyre in South Australia is the largest of Australia's salt lakes. At its lowest point the lake is 12 metres below sea level and covers an area of 9300 square kilometres in two basins. The lake once formed a vast inland sea in wet tertiary times. Now, however, it is usually dry and covered in salt pans, but it receives occasional waters from surrounding river and creek beds when it rains. The only recorded filling of the lake took place in 1950 when 8000 square kilometres of water surface formed, but it dried out in two years.

Although a great deal of land is available, much of it is uninhabitable because of lack of water and inadequate communications. This is reflected in the fact that less than 15 per cent of Australians live in rural areas.

▲ The Hamersley Range in Western Australia, noted for its brilliant reds and purples at certain times of the day, is characteristic of Australian mountain ranges.

▼ The Macdonnell Ranges, parallel ridges of bare, reddish rocks, extend for over 160 kilometres west and north-east of Alice Springs, in the Centre of Australia.

▼ This map, which shows Europe and Australia on the same scale, gives an idea of the vast distances involved in travelling in Australia. Australia covers 30 degrees of latitude, equivalent to almost the whole of Western Europe, and there is a wide variation in climate.

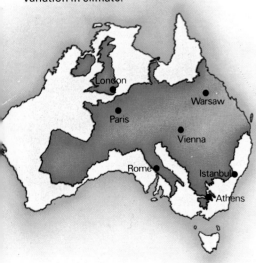

► A drover herds beef cattle across the Davidson River in Queensland, an area noted for the production of beef. Although cattle are usually moved to market by road train, the old method is sometimes still used.

▼ A view of Thredbo, New South Wales, in the Australian Alps, the highest land and only extensive alpine area in Australia. The area has more snowfields than Switzerland.

◄ Wandiligong, Victoria, a typical pastoral scene in an area of high rainfall near the south-eastern seaboard. Stud farms and sheep stations abound in this type of countryside.

Who are the Australians?

▲ The first Australians were the Aborigines. They are believed to have arrived in the north of Australia at least 30,000 years ago, probably across a "land bridge" from Southern Asia. They may have migrated in slow stages from island to island before much of the land was flooded by the sea.

▼ Although many aboriginals today have adopted European ways, those in remote areas still cling to ancient traditions, such as the periodic wandering known as "walkabout". Camels are often used by aborigines as a means of cheap transport.

First Australians

The first Australians were the Aborigines who are thought to have arrived at least 30,000 years ago, probably across a land bridge from Southern Asia. Their physical affinities are with people among tribal groups in Southern India, Sri Lanka and South East Asia. The Tasmanian Aborigines were a distinctive negrito group separate from the mainland people. They were wiped out by the white man and his diseases—the last Tasmanian Aboriginal died in 1888.

The first outside contact with the continent and its inhabitants came from Asian and possibly Arab seafarers and fishermen who visited the waters off the Northern Australian coast and probably landed from time to time in search of water and food.

European interest

The evidence of 16th century Spanish, Portuguese and Dutch mariners led to the development of the "Terra Australis" theory in the 17th century and the first real European interest in the continent.

The first recorded European landing was made by Willem Janszoon, Dutch captain of the *Duyfken*, on the east coast of the Gulf of Carpentaria. The spice trade brought other Dutch ships into waters close to Australia. Dirk Hartog and Abel Tasman played their parts in the discovery of the new land. Australia could quite easily have been settled first by the Dutch and later the French. The first Englishman did not arrive until 1688—William Dampier, the buccaneer, who was withering in his scorn of the north west coast. However, the British persevered and Captain Cook took possession for Britain of the eastern coast and named it New South Wales. The first European settlement was founded at Sydney Cove on 26 January, 1788, by Captain Arthur Phillip and his First Fleeters.

Building a nation

There were about 1,050 people in the First Fleet, and they were mostly male and British. About three quarters of these were convicts, most of whom were sent to the colony for very petty crimes indeed.

As time went by free settlers began to arrive from Britain, escaping from poverty and unemployment in the hope of a better chance. But the new life in New South Wales was far from easy.

In Australia today there are about $13\frac{1}{2}$ million people and about 20 per cent of these were born overseas. Although a large number of immigrants are of British origin, the population has become far more polyglot in recent years. Many people are of Italian, Greek and Yugoslav origin. Most other Western European nationalities are represented and there is a stable Chinese community, descendants of those who came out to work as shepherds and on the gold diggings. Since the abolition of the White Australia policy in the early 1970's, migrants of Asian, African and mixed descent have been accepted.

▲ Jack Farrell and his son are part of a dying tradition in Australia. Jack is one of the last "bullockies" left in Australia. These men were responsible for moving supplies and agricultural produce around the country in bullock wagons before modern transport.

Immigrants by Assisted Passage Scheme 1945–1971	
British	1,086,338
Dutch	98,233
German	95,569
Yugoslav	88,523
Greek	71,286
Italian	69,489
Polish	65,643

From 1945 to December 1971, Australia welcomed nearly 3 million settlers, including a quarter of a million refugees. The above figures show the numbers of immigrants by nationality who arrved in Australia under the Assisted Passage scheme. This system has largely been suspended now that there is no longer a need for unskilled manpower.

▲ British immigrants arriving in New South Wales in the 1880's. Until the "open-door" policy after 1945, most of Australia's citizens came from the British Isles.

◄ Although from very different racial backgrounds, these children are all Australian, learning to live in an integrated society.

▼ Since the so-called "White Australia" policy was abolished in the early 70's, people from Asia and Africa have been accepted as immigrants.

▼ The Chinese came first as shepherds but soon found work in the goldfields. They became very unpopular because they were so hardworking and did not mix readily with other European settlers. Laws were introduced to try to exclude them and the basis of the "White Australia" policy was established. There is still a thriving Chinese community in Australia. Many, like this woman in Sydney's Paddy's Market, are green-grocers and market gardeners.

The Australian character

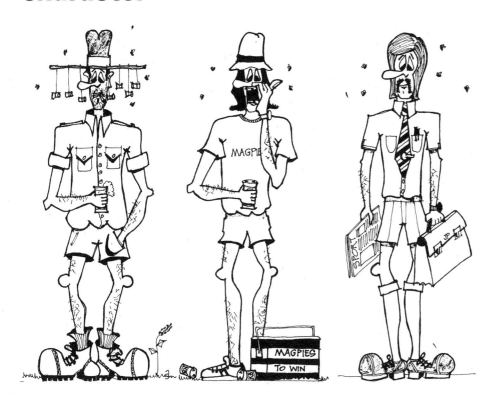

▲ Most Australians are dedicated city dwellers, usually living in suburbs like this, in row after row of red-roofed houses.

◄ How the Australians see themselves, or three common stereotypes of the Australian male. The outdoor type, or rugged bushman, with corks hanging from his hat, the rugby supporter, to be found at any major sports ground on a Saturday afternoon, and the city commuter, smartly turned out in shorts and long socks.

▼ Chips Rafferty, a famous Australian actor, personified the lean and suntanned bushman image, with which Australian men strongly identify.

Character and attitudes

Although the great majority of Australians live in cities, their character is strongly rooted in the bush tradition, born of a great and bitter struggle against an alien land. Australians are acquisitive and materialistic, friendly and hospitable, casual and often apathetic. They firmly believe in the principles of democratic equality and independence. All people are entitled to a "fair go" and an Australian will always sympathize with the underdog.

Although money is the greatest asset for social climbing, it is truly an egalitarian society. Success in public office and in business does not depend on accent, manners or dress and is open to all, not just the prerogative of the richer and well educated.

Australians are outgoing and usually cheerful, but they regard loyalty to their friends as being very important and can be over-sensitive to criticism of themselves and their country. Most people aim for a comfortable income and plenty of leisure rather than great wealth. Recent immigrants, or "New Australians", usually work much harder than the native-born Australians. People tend to move houses and jobs quite frequently and many young people travel overseas to "see the world" before they settle down to careers and families.

The image

The two most commonly recognizable stereotypes of the Australian are the "Chips Rafferty" bushman, the tall, laconic, weatherbeaten type, and the "Ocker" type as characterized by Barry Mackenzie, strident, pot-bellied and beerswilling. Both images have some truth in them but neither can be said to define the typical Australian. It is becoming increasingly difficult to do so, especially since the post-war immigration boom which injected a narrow culture with new and vigorous life.

Today, one in three Australians was born overseas or has at least one foreign parent. The lifestyle of most Australians reflects their British origins, but broader European and Asian influences are becoming increasingly important.

There have been three million immigrants since the last war, mostly from Italy, Greece and Yugoslavia. At first, ethnic groups tended to stay together in the cities, but the children of these immigrants are readily absorbed into the community. Since the suspension of the "White Australia" policy, more South East Asians have arrived. There was considerable Chinese settlement in the Gold Rush days of the last century, which has resulted in Chinese quarters in most cities.

▲ A scene typical of clubland anywhere in New South Wales. The Australians' love of gambling keeps the machines going day and night.

▶ Life in the consumer society. Australians love their home comforts and enjoy a high standard of living. This Spanish-style house in Brisbane with its swimming pool is of a standard which many Australians regard as normal.

▼ Two Australian characteristics which are often commented on. Immigrants work harder than established Australians. The competitive spirit is fostered—if not enforced—in young children by eager parents and over-zealous coaches.

Life in the cities

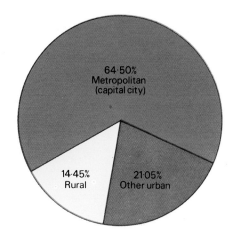

◄ Canberra, the beautiful, planned capital city of Australia, renowned for its blossom display in Spring and its magnificent autumn colours. It is the political and administrative centre of the country.

Pie chart:
- 64·50% Metropolitan (capital city)
- 21·05% Other urban
- 14·45% Rural

▲ A chart showing the large proportion of Australians who regard the city as home. The rural population is tiny by comparison.

▼ Sydney, the largest city in Australia, is built on the fore-shores of one of the world's most spectacular harbours. Its unique atmosphere and individuality stem largely from its ideal situation.

▶ A view of Melbourne across the Yarra River. The city is sophisticated and cosmopolitan and a centre for the arts and learning. It is now the third largest Greek-speaking city in the world.

An urban life

Australians are the most urbanized people on earth, yet most of them still stubbornly refuse to believe it and cling to the old image of the Australian as a bronzed bushman. Most people live in the same six coastal cities where colonization began, and more than two thirds of these in Sydney and Melbourne. Five of the six state capitals lie in latitudes equivalent to the Mediterranean and are all situated on the coast, where they are cooled by sea breezes. Australian cities are characterized by suburban sprawl with endless red roofs and gardens, but each still retains its own identity, ranging from the English-style Hobart in the south to tropical Darwin in the north.

The national capital of Australia, Canberra, is a planned city like Brasilia and Washington D.C. It was designed by Walter Burley Griffin and begun in 1913. A city of beautiful parks and gardens and the centre for political and administrative life, Canberra has also developed as an academic city of some standing.

A beautiful city

Sydney is the oldest and largest city of Australia. It is one of the most beautiful cities in the world, with a superb natural harbour and 22 splendid surfing beaches around its shores.

Melbourne, the long-standing rival of Sydney, is more of a planned city, with beautiful buildings and a great sense of civic pride.

Most of Australia's cities are situated on the south and east coasts, where they enjoy an equable climate. Perth, however, lies in glorious isolation along with Fremantle on the west coast, over 3000 kilometres across the continent and separated from the rest of Australia by vast deserts. Founded in the gold rush and still the fastest-growing state capital, it is a city renowned for friendliness and the sun. The other Australian cities, Brisbane, Adelaide, Hobart and Darwin all have a character of their own and provide a home for over 60 per cent of the population.

▶ Hobart, the capital of Tasmania, is the second oldest city in Australia. It is dominated by ships and the sea, and retains a charming, old-fashioned atmosphere.

Family life

▼ Home units, or apartments, crowd the beach front at Sydney. These blocks are becoming increasingly more popular as a means of providing family accommodation, although not all have such an idyllic setting! Many cities have also seen the rapid development of "cluster" housing (town houses) to meet the growing demand for more family accommodation close to town.

▲ Family and tribal ties are still very strong among the aboriginal population. Here, a family relax on the verandah of their home on the outskirts of Alice Springs. The contrast between the standard of Aboriginal housing and that of other Australians has been very great, but this is now being improved by the Federal Government.

▶ A typical Australian family timetable. Many Australians are up by 7.00 a.m. and have a shower before breakfast. The working day starts at 9.00 with a one-hour break for lunch. The family have the chance to be together in the evening, for dinner. Children then do homework and the family may watch television before going to bed.

High standards of living

Australians enjoy a very high standard of living by comparison with many other countries. Sixty-nine per cent of houses are owner-occupied and most married couples buy their own house fairly early in their married life. Eighty-three per cent of housing is in the form of detached, bungalow-style homes with at least one garage and their own garden front and back. Recently there has been a strong trend towards higher density housing in the cities. Home units, or apartment blocks, and town houses have begun to mushroom everywhere, the latter usually being set in landscaped gardens and with private courtyards.

The average home is fitted with many labour-saving devices and all types of kitchen and household appliances. This emphasis on material goods is similar to the North American pattern and indeed Australian consumer habits have been influenced by the American way of life.

Australian women are tending more and more to go out to work and now 41 per cent of married women work outside the home. There are very few domestic workers employed in Australia, since most people do their own housework and gardening.

▲ A typical Australian home: the red-brick veneer bungalow. It is surrounded by a well-kept garden and equipped with a double garage and all "mod-cons"

Home-centred living

Most Australians live in nuclear family units (parents and young children) in their own home. Sometimes, however, an extension or "granny flat" is built onto a house so that grandparents can live in close proximity but with separate living quarters. New immigrants to Australia often preserve the old-style extended family, at least for the first generation.

Family ties are usually strong and most families centre their activities as a group in the home. Australians entertain at home a great deal, especially outdoors in the summer. Many families have barbecues built in the garden as the centre for outdoor living, and a growing number have swimming pools as well. Home life is very informal. Friends drop in without being invited and many parties are spontaneous "open house" affairs. People tend to dress very casually and children usually go barefoot in the summer. Australians are renowned for their hospitality to strangers. Many friendships begin with a casual meeting on the beach, in a pub or watching a sports match, followed by an immediate invitation home to meet the family.

New country, old traditions

Freedom of religion

Australia has complete religious freedom, mostly of Christian faiths, but also of Muslim, Buddhist and others. There is no state or official religion.

Festivals of the Arts, such as Adelaide's biennial and Perth's annual attract top Australian and overseas performers. There are several big annual festivals of the carnival type including Melbourne's Moomba Festival, and the Vintage Festival in the wine-producing Barossa Valley in South Australia.

Christmas is celebrated in the traditional English way, despite temperatures in the upper register. Some Australians have indeed given this up for more appropriate cold meats and salads but most still cling to the old country traditions of turkey and Christmas pudding.

The Australian Aborigines have a rich store of ceremony and mythology. This is portrayed in rock and bark paintings and in ceremonial dances. Myths and legends are directly related to the religious life of the tribe. Most concern the origin of the world and history of human beings and natural species. The stories tell about the wanderings of the great Ancestral Beings, their deeds and many adventures. There is variation in the tales from area to area, but most have a great deal in common. Magic, especially, occurs in every aspect of life, particularly to uphold laws and customs.

Anzac and migrant traditions

The word Anzac stands for Australia and New Zealand Army Corps. Every year Anzac Day is commemorated the length and breadth of the country in remembrance of the Gallipoli invasion by Australia and New Zealand troops in 1915. For the older generation of Australians the Anzac legend is a symbol of their country: it celebrates courage and tenacity in the face of terrible odds. Probably the only true national day for many Australians is Anzac Day.

Migrant groups have introduced many colourful traditions into the Australian way of life. Some of these are the German festival, Hahndorf, in South Australia, the Scottish Highland Games, the Italian and Greek Blessing of the Fishing Fleet Ceremonies and the Chinese New Year. The traditions common to the Christian world are celebrated in much the same way as they are in many European countries. At Easter there are chocolate and painted eggs for everyone, and New Year is celebrated with rowdy all-night parties, dancing in the streets and firework displays.

A uniquely Australian festival, which can occur at any beach in the summer, is the Surf Carnival. This is a spectacular and highly competitive display of the skills of the many surf-lifesaving clubs whose volunteer members patrol Australian beaches rescuing the drowning and giving shark alarms.

▶ Aborigines in ceremonial body paint take part in a *corroboree* or ritual song and dance festival, in which myths and legends are re-enacted.

▼ One of the floats in the Moomba Parade, Melbourne. This one represents the Austrian community.

▶ A Chinese ceremonial dragon dances in the street during Chinese New Year celebrations in an Australian city.

▲ Anzac Day commemorates the landing of Australian and New Zealand troops at Gallipoli in 1915. It is still an emotional occasion for older Australians.

Education

Conservative system

Australian education systems are modelled on the old British methods and there are high, though often conservative, standards. Schooling has previously tended to be fairly formal although it is now becoming more oriented towards the "progressive" ideals.

Education is compulsory between 6 and 15 years (16 in Tasmania). Many children attend pre-school or kindergarten and there are also radio and television pre-school programmes. Children go to primary school until they are 12 years old, then they attend secondary or high school until the age of 15 or 18 years. Tertiary education usually starts at 17 or 18. Four out of five children are enrolled in government schools which are free and often co-educational. Non-government schools are usually denominational and charge fees.

Each state has its own Department of Education which trains and employs teachers, builds and administers schools and sets and marks public examinations. Scholarships are awarded annually in all States to encourage children to stay on at school, mostly at secondary level.

Australia has 18 universities, and more than 80 colleges of advanced education where the emphasis is on vocational education. External or public examinations are taken at the end of high school for university, college of advanced education and technical college entrance.

Special schools

The School of the Air is a unique and very special educational achievement. This is run by each Department of Education for children who live in remote outback areas and are therefore unable to attend a normal school. Lessons are done by means of two-way radio, and correspondence and homework are usually supervised by the children's mother. Most School of the Air pupils are able to meet their classmates and teachers only once a year at a specially organized summer camp.

Recently pre-schooling became the special concern of the Federal Government when they adopted a policy of aiming to give each child at least one year of state-sponsored pre-schooling.

The school day begins at 9 or 9.30 a.m. and ends at 3 or 3.30 p.m. Children are regularly set homework and sport is an important part of the curriculum. The school year is from early February to mid-December. The long summer holiday is for 6 weeks, beginning in December, and two shorter holidays (2-3 weeks) divide the school year into three terms.

Education is regarded by most Australians as important, and an increasing number of students are choosing to remain at school beyond the leaving age. There is intense competition for the available university places and a great deal of stress is placed on academic achievement.

▲ Immigrant children of different nationalities learn English in modern language laboratories like this. There is an intensive programme of immigrant education throughout Australia.

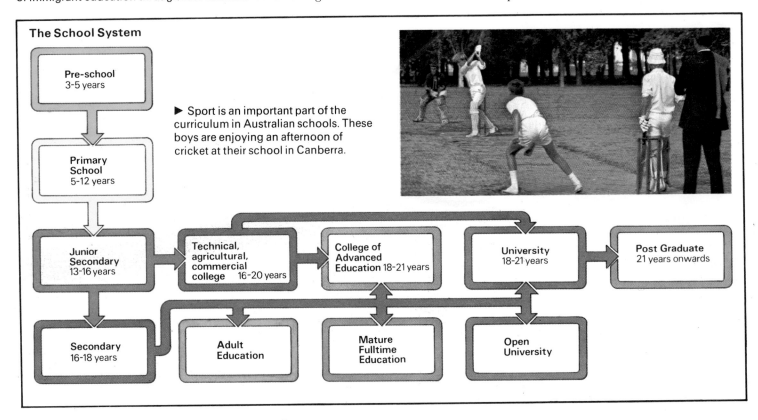

The School System

- Pre-school 3-5 years
- Primary School 5-12 years
- Junior Secondary 13-16 years
- Technical, agricultural, commercial college 16-20 years
- College of Advanced Education 18-21 years
- University 18-21 years
- Post Graduate 21 years onwards
- Secondary 16-18 years
- Adult Education
- Mature Fulltime Education
- Open University

▶ Sport is an important part of the curriculum in Australian schools. These boys are enjoying an afternoon of cricket at their school in Canberra.

▲ A pupil of the School of the Air concentrates on his teacher's voice during lesson time at Woodland Sheep Station, New South Wales. Lessons take up the morning, leaving afternoons free for homework.

► The pleasant climate enables many young Australians to do their lessons out of doors. These primary school children are having a geography lesson.

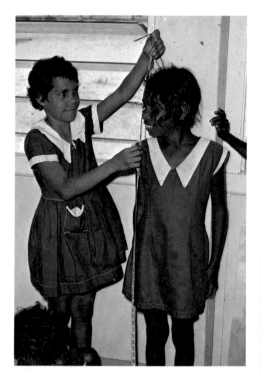

▲ Most schoolchildren wear uniforms. These Aboriginal girls at Yarrabah School in Northern Territory are having a practical mathematics lesson.

► An art class at a Sydney girls' high school. As well as academic subjects, most high school students choose different kinds of creative activities as part of their course.

Language and media

▲ Bookshops flourish in Australia, despite the fact that books are a very expensive commodity, compared with those in European countries.

Australian English has developed as a curious mixture with many aboriginal words, as well as Australian slang expressions, becoming absorbed into the language. Some of the more interesting aboriginal words have been retained as place names.

Arramagong:	wombats running into their holes
Bimbimbie:	many birds
Boolaroo:	many flies
Canberra:	meeting place
Collymongle:	long lagoon
Dandaraga:	good country
Derribong:	green trees
Goondiwindi:	water coming over the rocks
Grong Grong:	very hot
Illawarra:	high place near the sea
Laane-Corre:	home of the kangaroo
Murrumbidgee:	big water
Nindalyup:	crooked creek
Oodnadatta:	blossom of the mulga
Quirindi:	dead tree on a mountaintop
Urunga:	long beach
Waidup:	water all summer

▶ The older generation of immigrants are encouraged to attend adult education classes in English. This helps them to become integrated into the community.

Australian English

English is the national language of Australia, but there has always been a great readiness amongst Australians to use old words in different ways and invent new words. A vigorous and distinctive idiom has developed, as individual as that of the United States of America. There is little variation in accents from one place to another, despite the size of the country. A general division exists between "broad" and "educated" Australian, and between country and city forms of speech. Most people understand each other very well, whether from Perth, Darwin, Alice Springs or Melbourne, and there are no true class or regional dialects. Australians tend to express themselves in a very direct manner: they don't like to "beat about the bush".

The media

Free speech and freedom of the press are established values and the media are effectively beyond political control. The Department of the Media supervises most matters relating to information and entertainment media and Government publicity and information.

The first newspaper published in Australia was the "Sydney Gazette and New South Wales Advertiser" in 1803. There are now about 600 newspapers including 19 major dailies and 375 published outside the State capitals. There is also a flourishing periodical press and most English-language journals from overseas are available locally. Many ethnic journals have been launched in recent years to meet the demand created by migrant groups.

The Government-run Australian Broadcasting Commission (ABC) is operated on the lines of the BBC in Britain. Commercial radio stations and channels are operated by various companies under licence. There are 41 national and 45 commercial television stations covering the more densely settled areas. The standard of broadcasting has improved greatly in recent years and especially since the introduction of colour television in early 1975.

Film

The first Australian-made film was of the Melbourne Cup in 1896. The Australian film industry thrived from 1905 to the 30s, only to wind down just before the war through lack of finance. There have been some excellent Australian films in recent years such as *Wake in Fright* and the recently acclaimed *Picnic at Hanging Rock*.

▲ This news stand on a Sydney street corner shows the variety of foreign-language newspapers available. Although living in a new country, immigrants like to maintain old cultural links.

► An Australian Broadcasting Commission film crew reporting on a surf carnival for a television news programme.

▲ Stamp designs record recent historical events as well as other aspects of Australian culture and geography.

► More than 630 newspapers, including 58 dailies, are published throughout Australia. Periodicals range from the high-circulation women's magazines to small specialized journals.

Shopping

▲ A fruit stall in Paddy's Market, Sydney. This unique, under-cover market sells everything from live ducks to second-hand clothes.

◄ Norseman, a small town in Western Australia, where wide awnings and verandahs give an air reminiscent of the Wild West. Shops range from saddlers to general provisions and supermarkets.

▲ The fast-food industry is well developed in Australia, modelled on American ideas. Pizza parlours and hamburger bars abound in most towns and cities.

▼ Dixon Street, Sydney, in the heart of Chinatown, a fascinating area full of Chinese grocery shops, restaurants and gaming clubs.

Huge shopping complexes

Shops and stores in Australia are not very different from those in other parts of the Western world. They stock a wide variety of imported and Australian-made goods and many put great emphasis on efficiency and customer service. In the cities there are many large department stores modelled on the American and European equivalents. Shopping arcades, walking streets and plazas are now becoming popular and the capital cities have fruit and vegetable, meat and fish wholesale markets similar to those in Europe.

Newer suburbs and residential areas increasingly follow the American model of vast shopping complexes under one roof with huge underground or open-air car-parks. Many people do their weekly shopping in the vast, slick supermarkets where groceries are delivered to shoppers' cars before they drive out of the carpark. More and more shopping centres are staying open late one night a week, but most stores close at 5 or 5.30 p.m. during the week, on Saturday afternoons and all day Sunday. However, in the suburbs, small grocery shops and delicatessens are often open for long hours all week.

In the cities, the variety of small shops is as diverse as the population itself. Continental delicatessens are often run by Greek and Italian migrants and there is an abundance of small cafes, few of which, however, are the open-air type, despite the climate. Milk bars and hamburger shops reflect the American influence in food, while pizza parlours, gelato bars (ice cream) and speciality shops are also now springing up.

Clothes boutiques and fashion shops help young Australians to keep up with the latest trends in clothes and the many wine bars which have been opened recently in the main cities encourage the swing towards drinking more Australian wines.

Pavement vendors and small street markets do not exist as they do in Europe, with the exception of a few flower and news-paper stalls and the occasional fruit barrow.

Awnings and country stores

Visitors to Australia often comment on the wide awnings projecting from the sides of almost all shops. These protect the shopper from the intense heat of the summer sun and rain, which in coastal areas in particular falls in heavy downpours of short duration which drench in minutes anyone not under cover.

Country shopping centres are usually old-fashioned in atmosphere with wide, tree-lined streets, diagonal car parking on either side of the street, shady awnings and verandahs. Beautiful wrought iron "lace" is still quite common on the balconies and verandahs of country pubs and stores. Some small outback towns still have drinking troughs and tethering rails for horses! In complete contrast, country shopping centres often have large bulk wholesale and freezer centres, as well as up-to-the-minute supermarkets. Shopping on a cattle or sheep station can often mean shopping for three to six months' supplies at one time.

▲ Fresh seafood is always available, especially in this wholesale fish market. A trip to this market guarantees today's catch.

► Roselands, an up-to-the-minute "shopping town" covering a vast area in Sydney. This huge complex provides every type of shop in air-conditioned comfort.

▼ The weekly visit of this "shopping train" enables the inhabitants of a remote settlement to stock up on provisions.

Eating the Australian way

▲ Wine bars have become very fashionable replacements for the traditional pub as a meeting place for the young in cities.

Food revolution

The past 15 years in Australia have seen a revolution in eating habits. Before the immigration boom of the late 50's and early 60's, plain, English-style cooking was the norm, usually lots of steak and eggs, seafood and roasts. Snacks, such as hot meat pies with tomato sauce or fish and chips (with lemon, not vinegar), were also popular.

Today most inner city shops in Sydney or Melbourne feature a greater selection of European delicacies than many European cities themselves. The quantity, quality and variety of restaurants available in cities and large towns is amazing. These range from Harry's Cafe de Wheels—a converted caravan selling hot meat pies with peas and sauce near Sydney's Woolloomooloo Docks—to sophisticated establishments serving haute cuisine to an elegant clientele. There are many speciality seafood restaurants and steak houses, two types of food for which Australia is justly famous.

A taste for the exotic

Of course, climate influences Australian eating habits. Fresh chilled salads are a regular part of meals in the hot summers, as are barbecued meats. As well as fish and shellfish, fruit in great variety is part of everyone's diet. Tropical fruit from Queensland such as pineapples and bananas is very popular. Kangaroo and buffalo steaks have now become a speciality of menus in north Queensland and the Northern Territory, where kangaroos are now farmed for their meat and skins. The main meal of the day is the evening meal. Only one hour is taken for lunch so most people eat only sandwiches or a light meal away from home.

Australian beer is famous the world over and is consumed in large quantities, but wine is rapidly catching up in importance as more and more Australians come to appreciate the fine quality locally-produced wines.

The Australian pub

The traditional Australian pub is like no other on earth! Sterile tiled walls and floors, "men only" bars and a clinical atmosphere destroy any pretence of being a nice place to meet for a drink with friends. Drinking in these establishments is a serious business, not to be mixed with women and conversation! However, the traditional pub is now giving way to something more like the cosy English version or the slick New York bar. The outback pub, often a rough wooden structure with verandahs squatting forlornly in the middle of nowhere, is still a fascinating relic of the old Australia.

Some special Australian dishes

Carpetbag Steak

▲ A favourite way of combining two of Australia's most popular foods, steak and seafood. A thick fillet steak is stuffed with fresh oysters, wrapped in bacon and grilled to perfection before being served with salad and jacket potatoes.

Pavlova

▲ This dessert is named after the famous ballerina and is a favourite, calorie-rich summertime treat. A circular meringue base is heaped thickly with whipped cream and topped with strawberries or fruit salad. Traditionally, it is then liberally annointed with passion fruit pulp, although strawberry syrup can be used instead.

Anzac Biscuits

▲ These biscuits were first made to commemorate the Anzac Gallipoli landing during the First World War. They are based on an oatmeal and coconut mixture and have a pleasant nutty flavour. Golden syrup and butter are added to a mixture of flour, sugar, oats and dessicated coconut. Drops of the mixture are cooked in slow oven till crisp and golden.

▶ Australian wine consumption has rocketed in recent years. Some wines are very fine indeed, and not too expensive, the best being kept for the home market. Beer is still a popular drink and is drunk ice-cold.

▼ Eating out used to mean eating at a bar such as this, selling fish and chips, hamburgers and milk shakes. Immigrants have now introduced a great variety of restaurants.

Make an Australian Meal

LAMB WITH PINEAPPLE

2 lbs boned breast of lamb, cubed
Flour
2 oz butter or 2 tbsps oil
2 medium onions, sliced
4 sticks celery
3 large carrots
¾ pint stock and pineapple juice
1 tin pineapple chunks or half a fresh pineapple if preferred
Salt and pepper

This is a tasty and economical way to use two of Australia's home-produced foods.

Roll the cubes of lamb in seasoned flour. Heat butter or oil in a large casserole and brown the lamb quickly on both sides. Remove and set aside.

Add the onions and fry until transparent, then add the celery, carrots and pineapple and fry gently for several minutes. Season to taste and mix in a little more flour to thicken, if required. Add the stock and pineapple juice and bring to the boil.

Return the meat to the casserole, cover and reduce the flame. Simmer for one hour or until the meat is tender.

Serve with rice and tossed green salad.

PEACH MELBA

Peaches, tinned or fresh
Sliced sponge roll
Whipped cream
Crushed nuts (walnuts or almonds)
Strawberry syrup
Cherries
Vanilla ice cream (optional)

This famous dessert was created in honour of Dame Nellie Melba, the Australian opera singer.

Place the slices of sponge roll on small dishes. On each, place half a tinned peach, or poached fresh peach, with cut side uppermost.

Spoon whipped cream into the cavity and pour over a teaspoon of strawberry syrup. Sprinkle with crushed nuts and decorate with cherries.

Ice cream may be used to fill the peach, with piped fresh cream as a decoration.

Holidays and leisure

Plenty of free time

Most Australians work a 5-day week and most are free to "do their own thing" all weekend and from 5 o'clock every evening. There are ten paid public holidays per year and most people have three or four weeks annual holiday. This means that there is a lot of time for leisure and entertainment.

Water sports are very popular because of the favourable climate and the proximity of most people to beaches, lakes and rivers. Swimming and sailing are very popular, as are surfing, waterskiing and fishing. Almost everyone learns to swim at an early age.

Many Australians belong to clubs such as the Returned Soldiers' League, Rugby League or other sports clubs. These provide restaurants, sporting facilities, nightclubs and varied social activities. The club is used in much the same way as an English pub, as a place for meeting freinds on a regular basis.

The outdoor life

For Australians, the climate, wide open spaces and natural attractions of the countryside favour outdoor hobbies and leisure activities such as gardening and "bush" picnics. Many people take advantage of the well-equipped campsites on the coasts and in the country to take camping and caravanning holidays. Popular vacation areas are the Queensland Gold Coast, which has a tropical climate and is similar to the South of France, the Great Barrier Reef, the Southern Alps for skiing and the "Centre", an area of desert in the middle of Australia around Alice Springs.

Australians are great travellers, and as well as the almost obligatory "grand tour" of Europe and the British Isles, many people are now saving up for package holidays in Asian countries and the Pacific.

Department of Tourism and Recreation

In 1972 a Department of Tourism and Recreation was set up by the Federal Government in an attempt to help Australians equip themselves to enjoy and enrich increasing hours of leisure. The Department has introduced a programme to develop multi-purpose sport and recreation complexes, parks and training courses.

▲ This ski resort in Perisher Valley in the Australian Alps is only one of several thriving centres for the big business of skiing. Thousands of skiers flock here to the European-style lodges for weekends and winter holidays.

▶ The clear warm waters and abundant marine life of the Great Barrier Reef provide an ideal setting for all water sports, especially snorkelling and skin diving.

▲ Sailing is a very popular weekend pastime for residents of coastal towns and cities. This picture shows members of the Middle Harbour Yacht Club near Sydney.

▲ The Australian coastline is generously provided with superb surfing beaches, such as Avoca Beach, above, one of the Pacific beaches of Sydney.

▼ Bowls is one of the most popular organized sports with the older generation. There are hundreds of bowling clubs in every town and city around Australia.

▼ Luna Park, under the huge pylon of Sydney Harbour Bridge, is a popular amusement park with young and old alike.

The arts

Vigorous cultural scene

The arts in Australia have gradually developed a distinctive Australian flavour, spiced with the influence of many different cultures. For a young nation with a small population, Australia's cultural achievements since the last war have been impressive, especially in the field of opera, ballet and art.

The Australian opera has fostered some of the world's greatest singing talents, and the Australian Ballet, under the artistic direction and leadership of Robert Helpmann, has achieved international acclaim as one of the most exciting ballet companies in the world.

Australian drama and literature are also beginning to find an identity of their own. Playwrights include David Williamson, whose plays *Don's Party* and *The Removalist* have achieved international acclaim, Ray Lawler, Michael Boddy and Alex Buzo. Australian bush ballads and poetry reflect the outback and the struggle with the land. Poets such as Adam Lindsay Gordon, "Banjo" Patterson, Kenneth Slessor and Judith Wright have written poetry that is evocatively Australian.

In 1973, Patrick White became the first Australian to win the Nobel Prize for Literature, and Thomas Keneally is also being recognized as another author of international standing.

New directions in art

Australian painters have created a distinctively Australian tradition in art. Artists such as Tom Roberts, Hans Heysen, Elioth Gruner and the Aboriginal Namatjira have captured the unusual beauty of the Australian bush. The paintings of Arthur Boyd, William Dobell and Sidney Nolan have achieved international acclaim. Australians are very keen buyers of original art and readily lend their patronage to would-be artists, who are well supported and far from "starving in a garret".

The Victorian Arts Centre in Melbourne houses one of the richest art collections in the world, while the amazing Sydney Opera House has the highest subscription rate of any concert hall in the world, and is in itself a remarkable architectural achievement.

▲ Djawa, an Aboriginal patriarch, works on his bark paintings at the Millingimbi Methodist Mission, Crocodile Islands, Northern Territory.

▼ The Australian Ballet school, which has produced such dancers as Garth Welch and Elaine Fifield, rehearsing a new production in Melbourne.

▲ Joan Sutherland is one of Australia's most famous opera singers. She was born in Sydney but now lives and works mostly in Europe and America. She has a magnificent soprano voice.

▼ A scene from the recent and very successful Australian-made film *Picnic At Hanging Rock*. The Australian film industry has enjoyed a revival in the 1970's and has found recognition in Europe.

▲ A detail from *Glenrowan* by Sidney Nolan, one of the most widely-recognized Australian artists. This painting is one of a series based on the famous Ned Kelly narrative. Nolan now lives mainly overseas.

▼ Patrick White has been acclaimed as Australia's greatest writer. Apart from an early period of his life as a farmer near Sydney, he has lived mainly in Europe. His works include *Voss* and *The Tree of Man*.

Discovery and exploration

▼ When the first white settlers arrived in the colonies, they found aborigines living much the same life as they had for centuries—a primitive and isolated existence.

▲ A 1569 Mercator's Projection map of *Terra Australis*—the imagined Great South Land. It was a combination of Portuguese, Spanish and Dutch mercantile exploration into Asia which finally proved its existence.

◀ William Dampier, the English pirate, explored the coasts of north-west Australia and New Guinea in his ship *Roebuck* in 1688 and 1699. Here he is shown examining a boomerang, but he described the Aborigines as "the miserablest people on earth" and the land as barren.

Aborigines

There were about 300,000 Aboriginal people in Australia at the time of the first European settlement. They were scattered in small, nomadic tribal groups across the continent. Most lived in the better-watered coastal fringes, especially the south and east. They did not cultivate crops nor domesticate animals but did bring with them a wild dog, later called the dingo. Material belongings were few but some of their weapons and tools were very ingenious. The boomerang and woomera (spear thrower) were Aboriginal inventions.

The tribes lived in defined areas of land, spoke a wide variety of languages, developed complex social systems and a rich culture of mythology and ceremony. The coming of the white man destroyed their way of life forever. They were hunted, abused and often killed and their land was confiscated.

The First Fleet

In 1770 Captain James Cook in his ship, the *Endeavour*, sighted and charted the east coast of Australia. He sailed on through the Torres Strait and finally landed on Possession Island, two miles off Cape York, where he hoisted the Union Jack and claimed the east coast for Britain.

On the 26th January 1788 the penal colony of New South Wales was founded at Sydney Cove. The First Fleet of eleven ships was commanded by Captain Arthur Phillip and brought 760 convicts and 270 soldiers and sailors.

Exploration and the goldrush

The first settlement thrived, and more were soon established, but it was 25 years before a way was found through the Blue Mountains west of Sydney to the great expanse of fertile plains beyond. A route was finally discovered by Blaxland, Lawson and Wentworth. This great achievement was followed by those of other explorers including Evans, Oxley, Hume and Hovell, Sturt, Mitchell, Stuart, Leichhardt and Forrest, who probed into the interior in all directions.

Gold was discovered for the first time by Edward Hargraves at Bathurst, New South Wales, in 1851. This saw the beginning of a tremendous surge of immigrants into the colonies which tripled the population in ten years. Gold, wool from the Spanish Merino sheep and wheat from the vast plains were the building blocks of a new nation. The essential remaining ingredient to fulfil the promise was people and more people.

▲ A painting by Talmage, *The Founding of Australia*, showing Captain Cook hoisting the British flag to claim Australia for Britain.

▼ Governor Dayey's Proclamation to the Aborigines, 1816. He was responsible for bringing some progress and prosperity to the colony of Tasmania, which he found in a state of miserable disorder. Typical of many early colonial administrators, he was less than honest and lived a debauched life. This photograph was taken from the original board in the Mitchell Library, Sydney.

▼ The explorers Burke and Wills leave Melbourne on their ill-fated expedition to cross the continent from south to north.

The making of a new land

▲ Early settlers clearing the hostile bush to build their first home, in most cases a wattle and daub hut with few comforts.

▼ A family of early settlers. Theirs was a constant battle against appalling odds. People who survived this harsh life were a tough breed.

"Up for grabs"

Early governors had power to make free grants of land to anyone, whether emancipated convict, military man or free settler, who was willing to employ, feed and clothe convicts. "Selectors" were people who, through Lands Acts passed in New South Wales and Victoria after 1860, were given the opportunity to "select" land to turn into a farm. Most failed to make a living, lacking experience and money to fight a hostile environment and infertile soil. Failure to maintain the 3-year payment for the land, plus corruption led to many "selections" being taken over by the "squatters".

Squatters were people from every walk of life, from ex-convicts to members of the English aristocracy. They went west in the trail of the explorers and "squatted" on land of their choice. They built a slab hut by a waterhole and began farming, in the beginning owning only a few free range sheep and producing small quantities of wheat. Many failed dismally but others prospered and were the fore-runners of today's wealthy graziers, known as the "squattocracy". Squatters fought long for security of tenure and there were many clashes between squatters and selectors over the ownership of land. Australian folk culture grew out of this hard life.

Cobb and Co. and bushrangers

As Australia was opened up by the pioneers with their bullock waggons, roads were painstakingly carved out of the hostile bush. Eventually people began to need and demand a more efficient means of transport between settlements, and mail and supplies had to be got through as well. In 1853 an enterprising Californian called Freeman Cobb founded Cobb and Co. to provide coach transport to and from the goldfields in Victoria. He imported American stage coaches, swung on leather straps and capable of using the roughest tracks with some speed. These coaches made the name Cobb & Co. famous and dominated Australia's inland roads for decades.

With the stagecoaches came Australia's folk heroes, the bushrangers, who were often escaped convicts and mostly desperate and very unpleasant characters, whatever their popular image. The most infamous were Ned Kelly, "Thunderbolt", Frank Gardiner, "Black Dan" Morgan, "Captain Moonlite", Ben Hall, "Bold Jack Donohoe" and "Gentleman Matt" Cash. There was even a Chinese bushranger in New South Wales—his name was San Poo! These men lived a wild and dangerous life in the bush, robbing stagecoaches, holding up respectable citizens and terrorizing whole districts.

▼ This general store sign advertises that "gold is bought here". Many early miners also used gold as a currency in exchange for provisions.

▲ The arrival of the Geelong Mail. Communications and supplies were a real problem with the bad roads, great distances and threat of bushrangers.

▼ An old engraving showing bushrangers holding up a gold escort. This scene was all too common in the days of the gold rushes in New South Wales, Victoria and Queensland.

V. R.
£1,000 REWARD !!!
FOR THE KELLY GANG.

GO AND SEE
THE GREAT PICTURE
OF THE
NOTORIOUS BUSHRANGERS,
Painted by Fry from a photograph taken on the ground where the Murder of Sergeant Kennedy was committed. Every Visitor will be presented with a photograph of the Notorious Ned Kelly.
Now on View opposite Theatre Royal.

▲ A poster offering a big reward for information leading to the capture of the most notorious bushranger of all, Ned Kelly. He was finally hanged in Melbourne in 1880.

35

Beginnings of the young country

▲ Henry Parkes, who became a brilliant politician and was Premier of New South Wales five times between 1872-91.

Colonies to States

The early 1800's brought the beginnings of other colonies apart from New South Wales and these were later to become the six Australian States and their capital cities. By 1834 all the colonies were founded, but until the 1850's they continued to be administered from Britain through appointed governors. New South Wales became the first self-governing State in 1855 with a constitution embodied by an Act of British Parliament. Within five years, all but Western Australia, which retained administrative links with Britain until 1890, had followed suit.

The idea of Federation and a national identity took time to develop. Common interests such as the wool trade, questions of trade, tariffs and manufacturing, and rumours of French and German interest in the region, gradually led to a realization of a need to co-operate. The first draft of the Federal Constitution was drawn up in 1891, sponsored by Henry Parkes, Premier of New South Wales. The Commonwealth of Australia was declared on the 1st January 1901, followed by the opening of the first Federal Parliament on the 9th May 1901 by the later King George V. The first Prime Minister was Sir Edmund Barton.

The nation develops

The Franchise Act of 1902 gave a Federal vote to all men and women over 21 years. Australia was one of the first countries to give the vote to women and was the pioneer of voting by secret ballot for parliamentary elections. Australia was also the first country to introduce compulsory voting.

World War I greatly restricted communications and trade between Australia and Europe and the young nation had to fend for itself. Although she had only 5 million people, Australia sent 329,000 troops to war, suffered massive casualties and earned a high reputation. The economy suffered a severe setback in the Depression of 1929. Development of secondary industry saved the economy, especially iron and steel. World War II gave great stimulus to industry but created a serious labour shortage in primary industry which led to the "Open Door" immigration policy after 1945. Australia became the "lucky country" with opportunities for all comers. Ships came packed with hopeful, wide-eyed immigrants of 40 different nationalities.

▼ The Duke of York, later King George V, declaring the Commonwealth of Australia at the first Australian Parliament, Melbourne' Exhibition Building in 1901.

▲ The first Australian Prime Minister, Sir Edmund Barton, who inherited the political mantle of Sir Henry Parkes. He was totally dedicated to the cause of Federation and served on the Drafting Committee of 1891 and led delegates in the conventions of 1898.

▼ The immediate post-Federation period saw a vigorous campaign to encourage immigration to the newly-created nation. This poster in London is typical of the era.

▲ The poster campaign was particularly successful in areas of poverty and unemployment in the British Isles. These emigrants are leaving Liverpool in 1913.

▼ Australian and New Zealand Army Corps in action during the Gallipoli invasion of 1915. This famous campaign brought a new feeling of national pride to Australia.

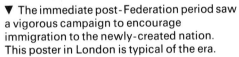

Life in the bush

◄ "The Alice" or Alice Springs, the main town of Central Australia, is the typical outback town. It is beloved in legend and literature and by all Australians, bush and city dwellers alike.

▲ A drover, mustering sheep, has picked up an ailing ewe to be taken back to camp for treatment.

Old ways dying

It is impossible to define the area known as "the bush" or the "outback": it is just anywhere the cities are not. The people who live in the vast spaces and battle against drought, bushfires, floods, heat, flies and bad seasons are of a different breed to the city slickers. They are instantly recognizable in a crowd.

Today, the old ways of the bush are dying. The legendary swagman or "swaggie" is rarely seen. Two-way radio has replaced the telegraph, light aircraft and road trains now take the place of drovers and bullock waggons and motor bikes and jeeps have replaced the horse. Freezers are now used instead of salt beef and a pantry full of preserves, and home generators and electric light instead of fuel stoves and oil lamps. Yet this is the world which evolved the Australian principles of "mateship" leaving bush ballads like *The Man from Snowy River* and the stories of bush heroes by Lawson.

A single cattle or sheep "station" can consist of thousands of square kilometres. The homestead, a cluster of dwellings, outbuildings, store and bush post office, is often 20-30 kilometres from the "front gate". The nearest neighbours are hundreds of kilometres away and people drive just as far for a party, picnic races or a cricket match. Mustering stock, shearing and dipping, the stock sales and the agricultural shows are the highlights of the year.

Flora and fauna

Unique flora and fauna evolved in Australia as the result of centuries of isolation from the rest of the world. Unusual wildflowers include waratah, Sturt's desert pea, flannel flower and kangaroo paw, while the commonest species of native trees are eucalyptus (gum trees) and acacias (wattles).

Many Australian animals are not found anywhere else in the world. There are special areas of natural bushland throughout Australia which have been set aside as national parks. These areas contain Australian plant and animal species, their habitats and landscapes which are of specific scientific, educational, recreational or aesthetic value.

Concern for the environment

Responsibility for the environment and nature conservation in Australia is shared by the government and individual States. Within the national parks the natural environment is protected and preserved and human exploitation or interference is kept to a minimum.

Most of Australia's animals are protected by law and must not be killed, captured or held without permission of the appropriate wildlife authority. Regulations on hunting, fishing and the use of firearms vary from State to State but in all cases these are designed to ensure the continued protection of native wildlife.

▲ Aboriginal stockmen "boil the billy" and make "damper" (unleavened bread). This was, with "bully" or salt beef, the staple diet of bushmen on the road in days gone by.

▲ No-one envisaged in the days of Cobb and Co. that the vast Australian distances would one day be easily managed with air taxis, small private planes and a network of efficient air transport.

▶ One of the events of the bushmen's year is usually the rodeo and picnic race meeting, which takes place on a cattle or sheep station with access to an air strip. People drive and fly from hundreds of kilometres around to watch their favourites compete. The rodeo was introduced to Australia from the U.S.A.

Animals of the Outback

Nearly half the native mammals of Australia are marsupials—they produce their young in a premature state and suckle them in a pouch until they are mature enough to fend for themselves. Some of the best known marsupials are the kangaroos and wallabies, the koala and the possums.

Less well known are animals such as the wombat, a compact stockily-built burrowing animal which looks like a cross between a badger and a small bear. The marsupial mole is a small, sightless burrowing animal which lives almost all its life underground. The

Duck-billed platypus

numbat or banded termite-eater is a small furry animal with an extensile, tubular tongue for eating termites.

Marsupial mice and rats resemble rodents except for the pouch and the lack of a rodent's long incisors. There are also marsupial or native cats, including a whole range of tree and ground dwelling weasel-like to cat-like animals.

The most extraordinary creatures of all

Koala Bear

are the monotremes, animals with a single vent for excretion and reproduction which lay eggs and yet suckle their young. It is now believed that they evolved from a distinct group of reptiles and are not related to the marsupials or higher mammals.

The two monotremes are the spiny ant-eater, covered in quills (like a hedgehog) with a tube snout and a long tongue for eating insects, and the platypus, an amphibious animal with a furred body, duck-like bill, webbed feet and a tail like that of a beaver.

Some of the most interesting and unusual birds of Australia are the emu, a flightless bird of similar size and appearance to the ostrich; the kookaburra, sometimes called the Laughing Jackass because of its noisy call like mocking laughter (it is the world's largest kingfisher) and the lyrebird, a very shy bird with a beautiful tail shaped like a lyre.

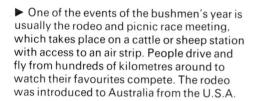
Kangaroo

Emu

Trade and industry

▲ Mount Tom Price in Western Australia is the site of a modern iron mining town built since 1965. The mine is open-cut using highly mechanized methods.

▼ A timber truck carrying karri and jarrah logs from the logging camp to a sawmill at Pemberton, Western Australia.

Industrial growth

The past 20 years have seen great changes in Australian industry. Manufacturing has become the biggest source of productive output and one of the most important employers of labour—the manufacturing industries employ about a quarter of the workforce.

Major areas of growth have been iron and steel manufacture, motor vehicles, electrical equipment and appliances, heavy engineering, oil refining, chemicals, textiles and clothing, food processing and the paper and pulp industries.

Overseas trade is vital to this island nation's economy. The development of secondary industry has been made possible by income from exports, mainly of primary products.

Imports have increased dramatically, two thirds of these being used by manufacturers as many more consumer goods are produced in Australia. Japan is now Australia's biggest customer, especially for wool, iron ore and coal. Large amounts of wheat have been shipped to China since 1960 and the U.S.A. has now replaced Britain as the main source of imports. The amount of trade with Britain has dropped dramatically since Britain entered the EEC.

Vast resources

Australia has enormous mineral deposits and minerals now account for about one quarter of all exports. Recent finds of immense deposits of iron ore, bauxite, nickel, manganese, copper, uranium, black coal, lead and zinc, as well as oil and natural gas, have thrust the country into world prominence as a source of basic raw materials.

Coal production, especially, has increased dramatically, providing high-quality coal for the coke ovens and other major heavy industries. A great deal is exported, however, to Japan and the U.S.A. via new port facilities.

Australia is self-sufficient in most minerals. Despite lower yields as mines are worked out, Australia is still sixth in world gold production.

Trade unions

Australia is a highly unionised country. Fifty-four per cent of all wage and salary earners belong to a trade union, of which there are over 294, and which hold considerable power. The dock labourers or "wharfies", on whom most of the economy depends, have several times brought the country to a standstill when their union called them out on extended strike.

▲ The first Australian commercial oilfield was found at Moonie, west of Brisbane, where production began in 1964. Natural gas was also first discovered in Queensland and Brisbane was the first city to be supplied with it. The total output of Australian oil in 1971-72 was 120 million barrels, about 70 per cent of needs.

▲ Inside a peach canning factory in the Murrumbidgee Irrigation Area, one of the most important fruit growing areas. A great deal of canned fruit is exported.

◄ An aerial view of the Port Kembla iron and steel complex. There are rolling mills, coking ovens, steel works and port installations.

▼ Inside the B.H.P. Steelworks, showing rolled steel production. The B.H.P. group of companies dominates the private sector of Australian industry.

A sporting nation

▶ Cricket has always been a popular sport in Australia and she has always fielded a very strong team on the international scene. One of the most recent and spectacular success stories has been that of Jeff Thomson, the fast bowler, pictured here.

▲ Evonne Goolagong (now Cawley) is the first Australian Aborigine to become an international tennis star. Her lack of temperament and ready smile have done much for her sport and her people.

▼ Horse racing is one of the most popular spectator sports. This photograph shows the Gold Cup Country Race Meeting at Wagga Wagga, New South Wales. Country racing is treated as a day out for all the family.

This sporting life

Australia's sporting champions have been many and varied and there are few popular sports in which Australia has not gained international recognition. Every weekend, Australians spend much of their time participating in and watching every imaginable sport from cricket and football to golf, surfing, horseracing and tennis. Sport is important in school life where at least one half day a week is set aside for competitive sport. It is competitive sport at which Australians particularly excel. There is an aggressive desire to win in most Australians. It is this, combined with the climate and spaciousness of the country that has produced an almost constant stream of world class sportsmen and women, out of all proportion to the size of its population.

It has been said that Australians will bet on anything and this is probably true. The building of Sydney's Opera House was financed by lotteries and the entire continent comes to a complete halt when the Melbourne Cup is run each year. The national pub pastime of "two-up" is no more than simple gambling: coins are thrown into the air while bets are placed on which side comes down face-up!

The art of spectating

All the traditional sports are highly popular both for participants and spectators alike. However, the art of spectating is highly developed in Australia—another excuse to get out and sit in the sun! Crowds of more than 100,000 are common at Australian Rules football finals in Melbourne, where the game was invented. Cricket Tests attract record crowds every time, especially with names like Lillee and Thomson on the scoreboard.

Recently sports such as squash, skin diving, water-skiing and surfboard riding have become popular. Snow skiing is very fashionable and it has become big business with the development of European-style ski resorts. There is plenty of scope for development as Australia has larger snowfields than the whole of Switzerland. Australia also claims to have started the world's first ski club at Kiandra, New South Wales in 1862.

A distinctively Australian sport is the volunteer surf lifesaving movement which looks after swimmers in the surf.

Picnic races and rodeos are favourite sports in the outback. People come from as far away as 600 kilometres to watch and bet on their favourites.

Some Famous Australian Sports Personalities

▼ **Margaret Court** An outstanding woman tennis player. She was Wimbledon champion in 1963, 1965 and 1970; Australian champion eleven times to 1973; U.S.A. champion 1962, 1965 and 1969-71. In 1970 she won the Australian, French, Wimbledon and U.S. titles, a feat accomplished only once before by a woman, in 1953 by Maureen Connolly.

▲ Australian Rules football is a unique development of rugby football and the leading spectator sport in Australia. Finals matches in Melbourne attract up to 120,000 people. It is an 18-a-side game with spectacular, high-leaping fast play.

▲ **Jack Brabham** Brilliant racing driver and car designer, he was world racing champion 1959, 1960, 1966. In 1966 he won the World Championship with his own car design, the Repco Brabham, the first racing driver to achieve this. He now lives in England, where he continues to enjoy both sports car and Formula I racing.

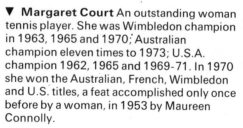

▲ **Rod Laver** Perhaps the greatest tennis player in the world. In 1962 and again in 1969 he won the Grand Slam of Wimbledon, U.S.A., Australian and French titles, as well as the German and Italian. He won Wimbledon in 1961, 1962, 1968 and 1969.

Farming the land

▲ Wheat harvest in the Wimmera District, Victoria. Wheat is the most important crop in Australia, second only to wool in the country's exports. Yields are constantly improving.

▼ A merino sheep sale near Mildura, Victoria. The merino sheep was bred in Australia for its fine wool, which contributes 75 per cent of the wool clip. Australia is the world's major producer and exporter of wool.

A rich land

Australia is a major producer and exporter of rural products. She leads the world in wool production and is a significant exporter of cereals, dairy products, meat, fruit and sugar. Ninety-five per cent of wool and more than 40 per cent of other primary products are exported. The country's prosperity was founded on primary industry and it has often been said that Australia "rode to prosperity on the sheep's back". Three-quarters of Australian sheep are merinos, bred from the original Spanish flock imported from the Cape of Good Hope in 1796.

Australia is also a major exporter of prime quality beef, much of which is shipped to the United States of America and Japan.

Vast areas of dry inland country support large flocks of sheep and herds of beef cattle. This is the pastoral zone with usually less than 380 mm of water a year. Shortage of water and suitable pasture has set limits on the expansion of this area. Wheat and other cereals are grown in areas of 380-640 mm rainfall per year, and wheat is usually grown in conjunction with sheep.

Well-watered coastal plains carry dairying, fruit, cane sugar, vegetables and sheep. Irrigation land produces rice, grapes and citrus fruits and recently cotton has become an important irrigation crop, especially in the Ord River Scheme in Western Australia.

Forestry, fish and wine

Australia carries about five per cent of commercial or potentially commercial native forest in its whole area. Most of the main commercial belts are found in coastal and coastal highland areas. As well as timber, forests supply oils such as eucalyptus, which is the most important, tannins and honey.

The Australian fishing industry is relatively small but growing rapidly. She is now an important exporter of marine produce, mainly rock lobsters, prawns, oysters, abalone and scallops.

The wine industry is thriving. South Australia produces 70 per cent of Australia's excellent wines as well as Australian brandy, which is produced in the sunny Murray River Valley. The really high-quality wines come from the rain-watered and not the irrigated vineyards, and the quality of Australian wine can always be guaranteed because summers are more reliable than in Europe. Most high-quality wines are consumed in Australia, and are not for export.

► There are 18 million beef cattle in Australia, and they are bred on vast, unfenced runs. The animals are mustered for branding, dipping and slaughter, but run wild for most of the time.

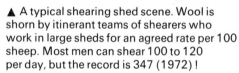

▲ A typical shearing shed scene. Wool is shorn by itinerant teams of shearers who work in large sheds for an agreed rate per 100 sheep. Most men can shear 100 to 120 per day, but the record is 347 (1972)!

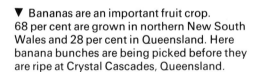

▼ Bananas are an important fruit crop. 68 per cent are grown in northern New South Wales and 28 per cent in Queensland. Here banana bunches are being picked before they are ripe at Crystal Cascades, Queensland.

Underground water sources are vital to this arid land. Ground water comes to the surface as a spring or can be reached with a well. Artesian water is under hydraulic pressure from an uphill direction sufficient to bring i to the surface at a bore. Sometimes a pump is needed to get the water up.

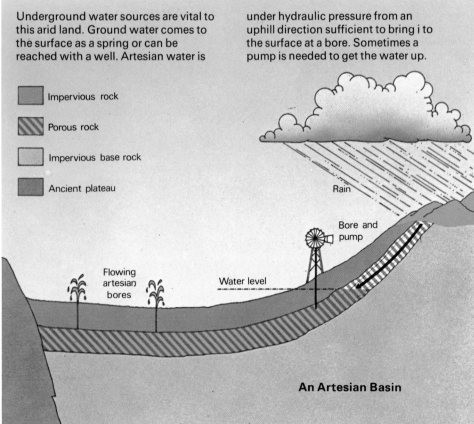

Impervious rock

Porous rock

Impervious base rock

Ancient plateau

Rain

Bore and pump

Flowing artesian bores

Water level

An Artesian Basin

▲ This train standing in Kuranda Station, Queensland, is typical of those found on suburban routes all over Australia.

◀ A Qantas Jumbo jet taking off. Qantas is one of the oldest airlines in operation and also has one of the best safety records. It was founded in Queensland in 1920 with two small planes.

On the move

Australia is a highly mobile society. People in the outback think nothing of driving 400 to 500 kilometres to a party or picnic race meeting, and it is common enough for city dwellers from Melbourne and Sydney to drive similar distances for a weekend's skiing in the Snowy Mountains or to an important sporting event.

Australia is one of the most highly motorized countries in the world. There are 440 motor vehicles for every 1000 people. Road accidents are a serious economic and social problem. Strict safety regulations for cars and compulsory seat-belt wearing have been introduced in an attempt to reduce the death toll. Cars clog the city streets and traffic jams are an ever-increasing nuisance.

Buses are the main form of city transport. There used to be trams in most cities but only Melbourne has retained these. Sydney has had an underground railway system for 50 years, the only one in Australia until Melbourne underground opened in 1975.

Spanning a continent

Railways are the responsibility of State and Federal Governments jointly and vast sums of money have been spent updating and extending the rail system. The standard gauge main line between the east and west coasts has recently been completed providing an unbroken connection between Perth and Sydney, Brisbane and Melbourne. The longest stretch of straight trainline in the world runs for 475 kilometres, from near the Victorian border across the Nullarbor Plain to near Adelaide in South Australia.

Distance no object

Despite the vast distances of the outback, the transport needs of the people who live there are well served by air, radio and the road movement of mail and supplies. There are now sealed roads along most of the main routes across the inland. The use of road trains (huge trucks towing as many as 4 or 5 trailers) to transport goods and stock has shrunk the distances to markets.

The air distance from Sydney to Perth is greater than from Amsterdam to Damascus or from Singapore to Tokyo, so it is obvious why Australia relies heavily on air services and private planes to transport people and freight across and around the continent. There is an extensive domestic aviation network and small planes have been adopted as a major form of private transport in the outback. Most cattle and sheep stations have their own airstrip and plane. There are two major domestic airlines: Trans-Australia Airlines, which is government-owned, and Ansett Airlines. Qantas Airways is the government-owned international airline. Now a worldwide concern, it was founded in Queensland in 1920 with two small planes.

The flying doctor

The flying doctor service is unique to Australia. Founded in 1928 by the Rev. John Flynn of the Australian Inland Mission, the service made it possible to bring doctors to patients and patients to hospital in the outback. The doctors and planes provide a life-giving service to the remote Australian inland.

▲ Most Australian cities had extensive networks of tramlines but Melbourne is the only city to have retained these.

▼ The main outlet to the northern suburbs and North Shore from Sydney is the new multi-lane Warringah Expressway from the northern approaches of the Harbour Bridge.

▲ One of the recent and most important innovations in the movement of stock and goods across the endless plains of inland Australia has been the road train. In this picture the truck is hauling three long trailers laden with cattle for market.

▶ Traffic in Sydney harbour is varied and constant. Here we see the famous passenger ferries plying between their many destinations across the harbour.

▼ People in outback Australia are dependent upon services such as that of the Flying Doctor which enables a sick person on a remote homestead to gain access to medical care quickly and safely.

Science and technology

A talent for pioneering

The most important achievements in science in Australia have been in the fields of agriculture and medicine. Notable contributions have been made through the work of the Commonwealth, Scientific and Industrial Research Organization (CSIRO). They have done valuable research into the deficiencies of Australian soils which are lacking in certain essential elements for plant growth.

Australian medical researchers have been awarded Nobel Prizes for their contributions to medical knowledge. Howard Florey discovered how penicillin could be mass produced at a reasonable cost. Sir John Eccles was awarded the prize for his work on the human brain and nervous system. Sir Macfarlane Burnet shared the prize for his research into the study of viruses and their effect on man.

Some notable achievements

Australian aviators pioneered the world's air routes, and all the major oceans of the world were first flown by Australians with the single exception of the North Atlantic. One of the most outstanding world authorities on prehistory was an Australian, Gordon Childe. Australians have achieved acknowledged world leadership in the relatively new field of micro-climatology.

Australia has played an important role in space exploration, a natural progression from its pioneering work in radio astronomy. The radio telescope at Parkes in New South Wales, the space tracking station at Tidbinbilla near Canberra and the radio heliograph near Narrabri, New South Wales, are all important links in the world tracking and communications network. The Australian Weapons Research Establishment based at the Woomera Rocket Range

▲ The 64-metre wide, revolving radio telescope operated by the CSIRO at Parkes, New South Wales, is a vital contribution to radio astronomy.

has achieved some important results in research work on electronics and guided missiles. The Australian-designed and built pilotless target aircraft, *Jindivik*, was produced and tested at Woomera and is now used for training in several other countries.

One of the major Australian technical achievements is the Snowy Mountains Hydro-electric Scheme. This is a massive engineering project which has provided water for irrigation and the generation of electricity through conserving run-off from melting snow on the Australian Alps. The scheme consists of lakes, reservoirs and about 145 kilometres of tunnels and more than 80 aqueducts.

▲ Oil was discovered in Australia in the 1960's, and now millions of dollars have been invested in modern oil refineries.

▲ Australian researchers have played an important role in developing different types of shark repellents. This photograph shows a swimmer testing a sonar shark repelling device.

▼ Bert Hinkler, the brilliant Australian aviator and inventor, who capped an impressive career of long-distance and record-breaking flights with a record flight from England to Darwin in $15\frac{1}{2}$ days.

▲ The Bass Strait field, off the Victorian coast, is one of the most important oilfields in Australia. Gigantic oilrigs using sensitive scientific equipment continue the search for new reserves.

Australia and the world

▲ The first Labor Prime Minister for 23 years, Gough Whitlam strengthened ties with Japan. Here he is shown with Crown Prince Hirohito and his wife.

◄ Australian anthropologists working in Papua New Guinea, the former Australian Trust Territory.

▼ Australian-produced "Gouda" cheese being prepared for export to Japan. Since 1967, Japan has emerged as Australia's most important trading partner.

Politics and foreign relations

Australia is an independent country, a member of the United Nations and the Commonwealth of Nations. Australian foreign policy is now being focused on regional associations, that is, relations with Asian and Pacific countries. Australia also has strong links with Britain and the U.S.A., although these links are not as close as they were formerly.

Asia is the area of Australia's primary interest and concern, however. She plays an active role in the Economic and Social Commission for Asia and the Pacific (ESCAP), the Colombo Plan, the Asian Development Bank and the South-East Asia Treaty Organization (SEATO). She places high priority on strengthening involvement with Indonesia, her closest neighbour, and with Japan, her biggest trading partner.

Australia has established diplomatic relations with China and was one of the first countries to recognize Bangladesh. She has had considerable influence in Papua, New Guinea, her former territory, and will continue to have a close involvement with this country now it is independent.

Trade and raw materials

Australian prosperity depends greatly on the production of food, raw materials and minerals, so trade and marketing of these goods is vital. There are ten National Marketing Boards and a Department of Overseas Trade to develop export opportunities. Australia was the first country in the world to initiate a system of preferential import duties to help developing countries to compete with industrial countries for a greater share of the Australian import trade.

Australians and sport

Most people think of Australia as a great sporting nation before anything else. The main spheres of Australian influence have been in swimming, tennis, squash and cricket. Swimming coaches have produced dozens of top class swimmers with their revolutionary methods, many of which are now used by coaches in other countries.

Australia has long been one of the dominant nations in world tennis. The Australian record on the Centre Court at Wimbledon is little short of amazing and the Australian team has won the Davis Cup many times in recent years.

▲ Sydney is a major centre for international trade and, as can be seen here, her docks are always busy with ships of many nations.

▶ Young Aussies on the road with the ubiquitous camper van ! Many Europeans must feel that half of Australia is travelling around in these.

▼ Anxious and hopeful faces of Italian immigrants as they arrive on Australian soil for the first time. For many, Australia is the land of opportunity.

Changing face of Australia

An exciting future

Australia has become a country which deserves to be taken seriously on the world scene. Her people are becoming less insular and less complacent. The Australian-born population have had their attitudes and rather narrow horizons ruthlessly widened in recent years. The extraordinary political storm which put the Whitlam government out and the Fraser government in has resulted in a healthy growth in scepticism, particularly in those who are holding the reins of power.

Australians are far more involved in issues concerning the quality of Australian life, the environment and the exploitation of natural resources. The country has come a long way from the old days of "Terra Australis": the people have developed their own identity, despite isolation and a continuous struggle with a harsh environment.

Despite all the economic problems which have beset Australia in recent years as much as they have the rest of the developed world, such as galloping inflation, unemployment and industrial unrest, the country has become more realistic and more stable.

New directions

Australia today is rapidly changing and finding new directions. There has been a distinct trend towards closer ties with her immediate neighbours in Asia and a breaking away from the old relationships with Britain and Europe, and to some extent, the U.S.A. In the past, Britain and America have strongly influenced Australian attitudes, customs and international relationships. Now Australia is developing a more independent stance. There is a more relaxed and less self-conscious Australian image emerging.

Australia is geographically in Asia, although she is still culturally European, but now Australians are becoming fascinated by Asian cultures, arts and crafts. Asian languages are now being taught in schools, often instead of the traditional French and German. European immigrants have introduced their own tastes in food, leisure and cultural pursuits, gradually enriching the Australian way of life and adding a cosmopolitan air.

Political attitudes are also changing. The Whitlam Labor-government introduced many reforms, including equal pay and improvements in the status of women, a better deal for Aborigines and massive financial help for the Arts. Australia's national identity is finally emerging and the future remains an exciting prospect.

▲ With the strengthening of Australian trade and diplomatic relations with Asian countries there has been a burgeoning of interest in Asian handicrafts and artwork in Australia. This shows a fine selection of Asian goods for sale in a crafts shop.

▼ A stockman rounds up sheep on a motor bike instead of a horse, a very common sight in the bush today.

Political feeling intensified to a previously unknown pitch just prior to the elections of November 1975, which were precipitated by the action of the Governor-General, Sir John Kerr, in sacking the Whitlam government.

▲ In the 1970's there has been a strong interest in Aboriginal rights illustrated here by a famous demonstration in front of Parliament House, Canberra.

◄ Malcolm Fraser, the Liberal Prime Minister of Australia, who succeeded Gough Whitlam in December 1975.

▲ Australia Square, Sydney. Open-air cafés give a new, European look to many cities.

Reference
Geography and Government

LAND AND PEOPLE
Full title: The Commonwealth of Australia.
Position: Australia is an island continent, bounded in the east by the Coral Sea, Tasman Sea and South Pacific Ocean and in the west by the Indian Ocean.
Language: English.
Area: The total area is 7,682,300 sq. kms., about the same size as the U.S.A. without Alaska or Hawaii.
Topography: The coastline extends 19,320 kms. Australia is the flattest of all the continents—average elevation 300m. compared with world average 700m. The most important physical divisions are the Great Western Plateau, the Great Dividing Range and the Central Eastern Lowlands. Highest land is in the Australian Alps (Mt Kosciusko 2228m) and the lowest at Lake Eyre (dry salt lake) at nearly 12m below sea level.
Administration: The Commonwealth of Australia, a federation of six States, was instituted on the 1st January, 1901. The first Prime Minister was Sir Edmund Barton. The first constitution designated Melbourne as federal capital until the site for its present capital, Canberra, was chosen.
Population: At December 1973, 13,268,600 (6,612,900 females, 6,655,700 males).
Political system: Parliamentary democracy. Legislative power is vested in the Parliament of Australia, consisting of the Queen as Head of State, her representative in Australia (the Governor-General), the Senate and the House of Representatives. All States except Queensland also have upper and lower houses of Parliament. The legislative powers of the State and Federal Parliaments are defined by formal constitutions. Each State has a system of local government.
Armed Forces: Total 67,457 (1974-5). Australia's basic defence concern is the security of its territory and offshore resources. It has close defence ties with Papua New Guinea, the U.K., the U.S.A., Malaysia, Singapore, New Zealand, Indonesia.

Climate of Australia

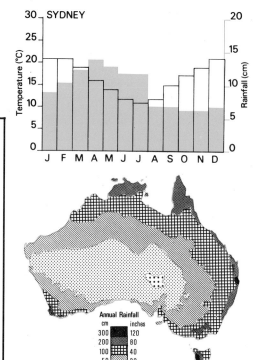

Annual Rainfall
cm	inches
300	120
200	80
100	40
50	20
25	10
12·5	5

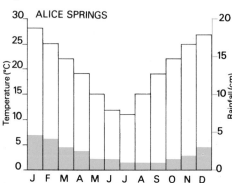

Australia covers more than 30 degrees of latitude so has a wide variety of climate. More than one-third of Australia is in the tropics. Snow falls on the south-eastern mountains in winter. Most of the continent has a temperate climate. The north is affected by destructive cyclones (e.g. Cyclone Tracey which destroyed Darwin on 25th December 1974). Australia is outside the earthquake zone, but much of the country is subject to severe droughts and floods.

Australia is a continent of sunshine: no capital city gets less than an average of 5½ hours of sun per day. Summer in the temperate regions is from December to February, and temperatures in these regions are hot in summer and mild to cool in winter. In the north there are only two seasons— wet and dry, and temperatures are constantly high.

Natural vegetation

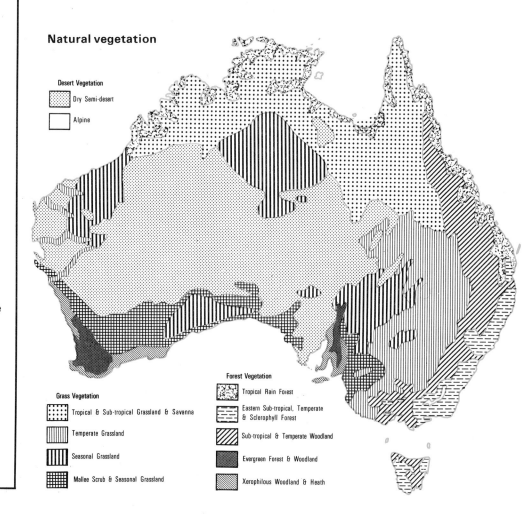

Desert Vegetation
- Dry Semi-desert
- Alpine

Grass Vegetation
- Tropical & Sub-tropical Grassland & Savanna
- Temperate Grassland
- Seasonal Grassland
- Mallee Scrub & Seasonal Grassland

Forest Vegetation
- Tropical Rain Forest
- Eastern Sub-tropical, Temperate & Sclerophyll Forest
- Sub-tropical & Temperate Woodland
- Evergreen Forest & Woodland
- Xerophilous Woodland & Heath

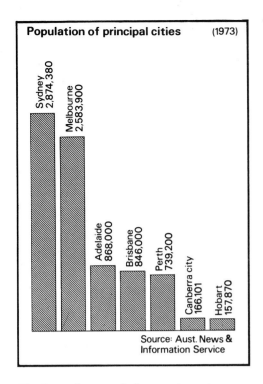

Population of principal cities (1973)

Sydney 2,874,380
Melbourne 2,583,900
Adelaide 868,000
Brisbane 846,000
Perth 739,200
Canberra city 166,101
Hobart 157,870

Source: Aust. News & Information Service

The population density

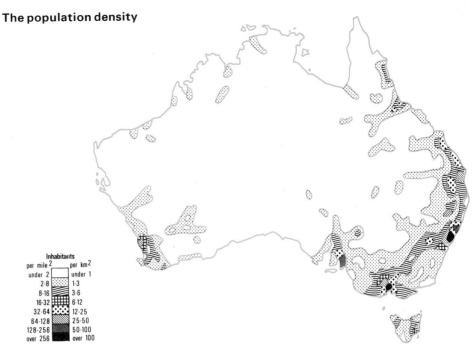

Inhabitants

per mile^2	per km^2
under 2	under 1
2-8	1-3
8-16	3-6
16-32	6-12
32-64	12-25
64-128	25-50
128-256	50-100
over 256	over 100

The Australian population numbers about 13½ million (estimate). Most people are of British and European origin. There are between 110,000 and 150,000 of Aboriginal descent. The total population has almost doubled since 1945. For its size Australia is very sparsely populated overall—average density per sq.km. was 1·7 in June 1973, against 24 U.S.A., 95 Europe (excluding U.S.S.R.), 229 Britain and 248 West Germany. The 1971 census showed 64·5% living in major urban areas, 21·05% other urban, 14·45% rural. The largest cities are the capital cities. The population is a youthful one: under 21 years—39%, 21–64 53%, only 8% in the 65 and over age group. Australia has had a controlled immigration policy since 1945. From October 1945 to December 1973 the net gain of permanent immigrants was 2·4 million. Eleven censuses have been held from 1881 to 1971.

The nation

Since Federation in 1901, Australia has been a federation of States with three levels of government: Federal, State and local. There is a system of representative and responsible government on the British model.

Australia, like Canada, retains close institutional ties with Britain and owes allegiance to Queen Elizabeth II of England, who is also formally Queen of Australia and Head of the Commonwealth. The Queen is represented in Australia by the Governor-General and six State Governors.

The Governor-General is formally the Head of State and the Chief Executive. In practice he acts only on the advice of the Prime Minister and his Cabinet, with the exception of the unprecedented action of the Governor-General at present Sir John Kerr, in dissolving the Labor Government of Gough Whitlam on 11th November, 1975 and forcing a general election.

The six State Governors have similar powers and duties to those of the Governor-General in their respective States. The division of powers between the Australian and State Governments largely follows the American pattern in specifying the powers of the national government and leaving all other powers to the States. The parliamentary system is divided into the three powers of legislature, executive, and judiciary.

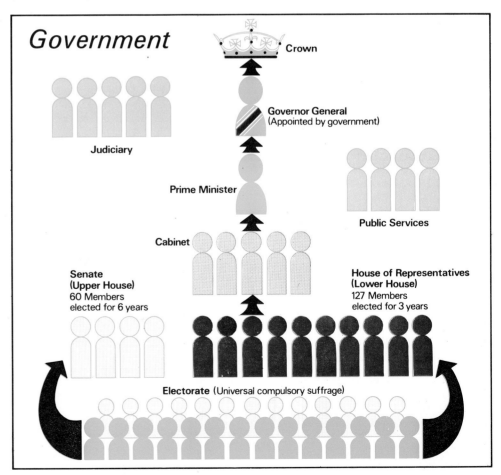

Government

Crown

Governor General (Appointed by government)

Prime Minister

Judiciary

Public Services

Cabinet

Senate (Upper House) 60 Members elected for 6 years

House of Representatives (Lower House) 127 Members elected for 3 years

Electorate (Universal compulsory suffrage)

Reference
History

B.C.

c.30,000   Aborigines arrived in Australia, probably across a land bridge from Asia.

A.D.
EARLY DISCOVERY
1606   Torres sailed through the Torres Strait between Australia and Papua New Guinea. Janszoon sailed into Gulf of Carpentaria.

1623   Carstenz charted western coast of Cape York.

1642   Tasman sailed around part of Tasmania.

1688   First Englishman, Dampier, landed on north-west coast.

1770   Captain Cook's first voyage to Australia.

1788   First Fleet under Captain Phillip arrived Botany Bay. Settlement at Sydney.

1796   Coal discovered at Newcastle.

1797   Merino sheep introduced from Cape Colony (South Africa).

1814   Creation of Civil Courts, Australia received present name.

1817   First bank—Bank of New South Wales.

1823   First Australian Constitution. Gold discovered, New South Wales.

1824   New South Wales a Crown Colony.

1825   Tasmania an independent colony.

1829   Foundation of Perth, Western Australia.

1831   First assisted immigration, to New South Wales.

1834   South Australia a separate colony.

1835   Site of Melbourne selected by John Batman.

1837   Settlement at Adelaide.

1841   New Zealand separated from New South Wales.

1854   Gold-fields riots, Ballarat, Eureka Stockade. First railway, Flinders Street to Port Melbourne (Victoria).

1859   Queensland a separate colony.

1871   Cable from Darwin to Java.

1878   Telephone introduced into Australia.

1894   Adult suffrage, South Australia.

1895   Free-trade Tariff, Land and Income Taxes, New South Wales.

1899   Boer War, Australian contingents sent. Federal Constitution Bill accepted.

1900   Old-age pensions, New South Wales. Proclamation of the Commonwealth signed. First Federal ministry.

THE COMMONWEALTH
1901   Commonwealth proclaimed at Sydney. Federal Parliament opened, Melbourne, by Duke of York, later King George V.

1903   Inauguration of Federal High Court.

1904   Commonwealth Conciliation and Arbitration Act.

1906   Wireless telegraph, Victoria and Tasmania. Papua taken over by Commonwealth.

1910   Penny post. Australian notes issued.

1911   First Commonwealth Census, population $4\frac{1}{2}$ million. Australian Capital Territory and Northern territory transferred to Commonwealth. Compulsory military training.

1912   Commonwealth Bank opened. First payments of Maternity Bonus.

1913   Foundation stone of Canberra laid.

1914   World War I—Australian forces embark. Double dissolution of Parliament.

1915   Landing, Gallipoli, 25th April. Broken Hill Proprietry Steelworks opened at Newcastle.

1916   Military Service Referendum defeated.

1917   Transcontinental Railway completed.

1919   Peace signed, 28th June. Sir Ross Smith and Sir Keith Smith made first aeroplane flight from London.

1924   Australian Loan Council formed.

1926   Imperial Conference, Dominion Status defined.

1927   Transfer seat of Commonwealth Government to Canberra.

1931   First Australian—Right Hon. Sir Isaac Alfred Isaacs, appointed Governor-General. Export prices fell to half 1928 level. Economic crisis.

1932   Sydney Harbour Bridge opened. Australian Broadcasting Commission formed.

1933   Acceptance of Antarctic Territories by Australia.

1934   Inauguration of England-Australia Air Mail Service.

1938   Introduction of new and more extensive defence programme.

WORLD WAR II
1939   World War II. National Register and Wealth Census.

1940   Australian Forces embark for overseas service. Petrol rationing.

1941   Outbreak of war with Japan.

1942   Darwin bombed. Battle of Coral Sea. Rationing of commodities.

1945   Cessation of hostilities—Europe, 8th May; Pacific, 15th August.

1947   Heard and MacDonald Islands transferred to Australia.

1949   New Guinea placed under international trusteeship. Snowy Mountains Hydro-electric Scheme commenced.

1951   Double dissolution of parliament.

1952   ANZUS Pacific Pact ratified. Formation of Australian Atomic Energy Commision.

1954   First visit to Australia of H.M. the Queen and H.R.H. the Duke of Edinburgh.

1958   Australia's first nuclear reactor opened at Lucus Heights, New South Wales.

1960   Social Services benefits to be paid to Australian Aborigines.

1962   Commonwealth Electoral Act amended to provide votes for Aborigines.

1963   Approval given to United States to operate a naval communications base at North West Cape, Western Australia. Nuclear test ban agreement signed.

1964   Northern Territory Legislative Council passed legislation to prevent discrimination against Aborigines. National Service Act passed.

1966   Australia adopted dollar-cent decimal currency. Immigration laws amended to provide for relaxation of restriction on entry of persons of non-European race.

1970   Voting age reduced to 18 years in Western Australia. Aborigines granted land leasing rights of Aboriginal reserves in the Northern Territory.

1971   South Australia lowered the voting age to 18 years. Australian troops left Vietnam.

1972   Women awarded equal pay in Equal Pay Case decision. Australian Labor Party elected to govern for first time in 23 years. National Service Act repealed. Australia established diplomatic relations with People's Republic of China and German Democratic Republic.

1973   The United Kingdom-Australia Trade Agreement terminated. All 18 year-olds given the vote. First national constitutional convention since Federation. H.M. the Queen and H.R.H. the Duke of Edinburgh visited Australia to open the Sydney Opera House.

1974   Serious floods in New South Wales and Queensland. H.R.H. Queen Elizabeth II opened the second session of the 28th Australian Parliament. Double dissolution of Parliament. First Aboriginal Special Magistrate sworn in at the Supreme Court. First woman Ambassador appointed. On Christmas morning the city of Darwin was destroyed by a cyclone.

1975   The Liberal-Country Party majority in the Senate blocked approval of the Budget for months. The deadlock broken by the very controversial decision of the Governor-General, Sir John Kerr, to dismiss the Prime Minister, Mr Gough Whitlam. This resulted in an election on 13th December which was won by the conservative opposition led by Mr Malcolm Fraser.

The Arts

ARCHITECTURE

Annear, Harold Desbrowe (1866–1933). The first significant Australian architect, rebelled against imported styles. Functional homes with features ahead of the times.

Blacket, Edmund Thomas (1817–1883). Leading Australian architect of second half of 19th century, chief exponent of Gothic revival. St Mark's, Darling Point, the Great Hall of Sydney University.

Greenway, Francis Howard (1777–1837). Between 1816–22 was Civil Architect to Governor Macquarie. A pardoned convict, he was the first Australian architect and one of greatest. Georgian style, St Matthews Windsor, St James Sydney, Hyde Park Barracks, Government House Stables.

Griffin, Walter Burley (1876–1937). Although an American, had great influence on Australian architecture. Designed National Capital, Canberra; Newman College Melbourne; a Dance Theatre complex, Melbourne; Leonard House and Capitol Theatre, Melbourne; community houses, Castlecrag, Sydney.

Grounds, Roy Burman (1905–). A pioneer of Australian interpretation of modern international style after 1934. Simple functional lines with Australian elements: verandahs, shutters, wide eaves, etc. Most famous works are the domed Academy of Science, Canberra, Melbourne Arts Centre.

Seidler, Harry (1923–). Inspired designer of domestic and office block architecture. Australia Square, Sydney; Blues Point Tower, Sydney.

ART

Boyd Family. Richly talented family who have had great influence on Australian art and culture. Most notable being Theodore Penleigh (1890–1923), and Arthur (1920–). The latter's work has made considerable impact both in Australia and overseas.

Dobell, William (1899–1970). One of the most outstanding figures in Australian art, best known as a portrait painter. His works have been described as forceful, highly perceptive. Classical style coupled with sardonic humour.

Drysdale, George Russell (1912–). Sensitive and compassionate artist, famous for interpretations of harshness of Australian environment. Lean, almost surreal figures in red and dusty landscapes.

French, Leonard (1928–). Leading contemporary artist noted for huge geometric abstract paintings on heroic or religious themes. Glass ceiling in Victoria Arts Centre, Melbourne.

Friend, Donald Stuart Leslie (1915–). Artist of international repute, influenced by living in Africa and Bali. Leader of an artistic group at Hill End, New South Wales, and of the later Merioola Group, Sydney.

Gruner, Elioth (1882–1939). An artist of the traditional landscape school. His work typifies the Australian scene and he managed to capture the special quality of the Australian light. *Morning Light.*

Heysen, Hans (1877–1968). One of the most famous of the early landscape artists in Australia. Noted for his paintings of the stark gum trees and vivid red rocks of the Flinders Ranges area, South Australia.

Lindsay Family. Perhaps the most talented Australian family, from Victoria. The most famous of the ten children was Norman (1879–1969), artist and writer. He is best known for his watercolours and illustrated children's books. Other Lindsay artists were Percy (1870–1952) and Lionel (1874–1961).

Nolan, Sidney Robert (1917–). Probably the best known Australian artist. Famous for series of paintings based on 19th century in Australia: *Ned Kelly Story, Burke and Wills expedition, Eureka Stockade.* Painted vast murals for 1972 London exhibition *The Snake* and *Paradise Garden.*

Roberts, Thomas William (Tom) (1856–1931). One of best artists of the Heidelberg (Melbourne) school. *Baled Up* and *Bourke Street Melbourne.* His works are full of vivid action and Australian atmosphere.

MUSIC

Hammond, Joan Hood (1912–). Achieved world fame as a dramatic soprano. She was also an excellent squash and golf player.

Heinze, Bernard Thomas (1894–). A leading figure in Australian musical world. Violinist, teacher and former Director of the New South Wales Conservatorium of Music. Best known as a talented conductor.

Melba, Nellie (Helen Porter Mitchell) (1861–1931). One of the greatest opera singers of all time, a great and colourful personality with a magnificent voice. She sang in all the great opera houses of the world but returned several times to Australia and founded a singing school in Melbourne.

Sutherland, Joan (1926–). An operatic soprano of highest international repute, she regularly appears at opera houses in Europe, America and Australia.

Williamson, Malcolm (1931–). Master of the Queen's Music, a composer with a worldwide reputation. Well known for his opera with audience participation. Works such as *The Stone Wall,* religious music.

LITERATURE AND DRAMA

Astley, Thea (1925–). Novelist and short story writer. *The Acolyte,* an award-winning novel.

Brennan, Christopher John (1870–1932). Considered by some to be Australia's greatest poet. Short, scholarly poems.

Dark, Eleanor (1901–). Leading novelist, best known for historical novels on the early colony. *The Timeless Land.*

Dennis, Clarence Michael James (1876–1938). Famous for humorous light verse ballads. *The Songs of a Sentimental Bloke.*

Hope, Alec Derwent (1907–). Leading modern poet and well-known critic. *The Cave and the Spring, The Wandering Islands.*

Keneally, Thomas (1935–). Important novelist and playwright. *Bring Larks and Heroes, The Survivors, Three Cheers for the Paraclete, An Awful Rose* (play).

Lawson, Henry Archibald (1867–1922). Probably Australia's best-known writer. Short stories of very high standard about bush life of period, ballads.

McAuley, James Phillip (1917–1976). Poet, critic and essayist. Followed 18th century and classical verse forms. *Under Aldebaran, A Vision of Ceremony.*

Palmer, Edward Vance (1885–1959). Novelist, short story writer, poet and playwright. *The Passage.*

Patterson, Andrew Barton ("Banjo") (1864–1941). Much-loved bush ballads. *The Man From Snowy River, Clancy of the Overflow.*

Slessor, Kenneth (1901–1971). Leading poet known for strong imagery and individual style. *Five Bells, Five Visions of Captain Cook.*

Stewart, Douglas Alexander (1913–). Prolific poet, dramatist and critic. *Glencoe, The Seven Rivers, Ned Kelly.*

West, Morris (1916–). Successful modern novelist. *The Devil's Advocate, The Shoes of the Fisherman, The Ambassador, Tower of Babel.*

White, Patrick (1912–). Widely recognized as the major Australian writer, with place in mainstream of English literature. *The Tree of Man, Voss, Riders in the Chariot, The Vivisector.* Brilliant writer and Nobel prizewinner.

Williamson, David (1942–). Playwright of international standing. *Don's Party, The Removalist.*

Wright, Judith (1915–). One of Australia's leading poets. Known for universal emotional appeal and clear, precise style. *The Moving Image, Woman to Man.*

Reference
The Economy

Trade and prosperity

Australia by world standards is a prosperous
country. Despite recent problems of inflation
and recession and previous periods of slower
growth, the economy since 1949 has
continued to expand in all major sectors.
This expansion has been accompanied by a
change in the structure of the economy: from
a country dependent almost solely on primary
production to a rapidly developing industrial
and manufacturing nation. In the past,
primary production accounted for 20–30%
of Australia's gross domestic product. Today,
this has dwindled to only 8%. About a
quarter of the workforce are engaged in
manufacturing industries, the most important
of these being iron and steel, motor vehicles,
electrical equipment, heavy engineering,
chemicals, oil refining, food processing,
paper and pulp and textiles and clothing.

Despite a declining share of the national
product, rural exports continue to expand.
Australia leads the world in wool production
and is an important supplier of wheat, dairy
products, sugar, and meat. 95% of wool and
50% of other primary products are exported.

Overseas trade is vital to the Australian
economy. Since the mid 1960's, minerals
have become a very significant part of this
trade. Major discoveries in this field have
brought the country into world prominence
as a source of vital raw materials.

Traditionally, Australia's imports were
mainly finished manufactures. Now they are
mostly producers' materials and capital
equipment—a direct result of the development of Australian manufacturing and
mining since World War II.

High standard of living

Australians enjoy a relatively high standard
of living: there are very few poor people in
comparison with most other countries. 67%
of houses are owned, and there is one car for
every three people.

A high percentage of homes have
telephones, television sets, refrigerators,
washing machines and other labour-saving
appliances.

Agriculture in Australia

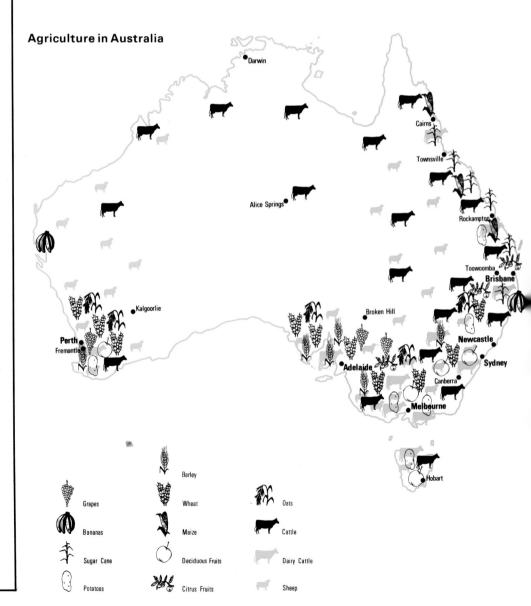

Grapes
Bananas
Sugar Cane
Potatoes
Barley
Wheat
Maize
Deciduous Fruits
Citrus Fruits
Oats
Cattle
Dairy Cattle
Sheep

Employment in Australia (1974)

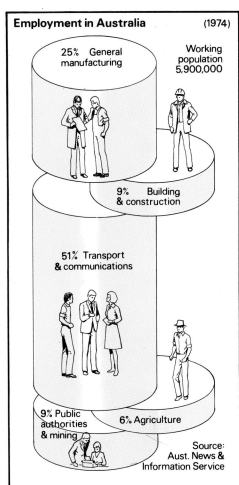

25% General manufacturing

Working population 5,900,000

9% Building & construction

51% Transport & communications

9% Public authorities & mining

6% Agriculture

Source: Aust. News & Information Service

In September 1974, the Australian labour force amounted to more than 61% of the population of 5·9 million. Until 1974 a level of unemployment above 2% would have been considered unthinkable. Today, with an inflation rate among the highest in industrialized nations, unemployment has become a real problem. The seasonally adjusted figures for June 1976 indicated an unprecedented rate of unemployment of 4·9%.

What is owned compared to other nations

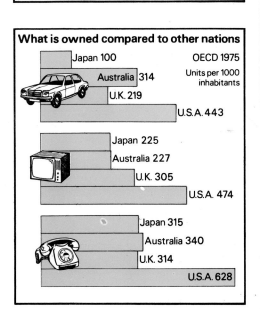

OECD 1975
Units per 1000 inhabitants

Japan 100
Australia 314
U.K. 219
U.S.A. 443

Japan 225
Australia 227
U.K. 305
U.S.A. 474

Japan 315
Australia 340
U.K. 314
U.S.A. 628

Industry in Australia

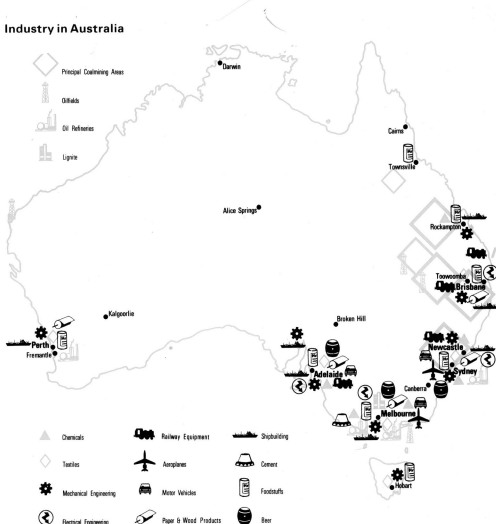

Principal Coalmining Areas

Oilfields

Oil Refineries

Lignite

△ Chemicals
◇ Textiles
✿ Mechanical Engineering
⊕ Electrical Engineering

Railway Equipment
Aeroplanes
Motor Vehicles
Paper & Wood Products

Shipbuilding
Cement
Foodstuffs
Beer

Imports and exports (Value in millions of dollars)

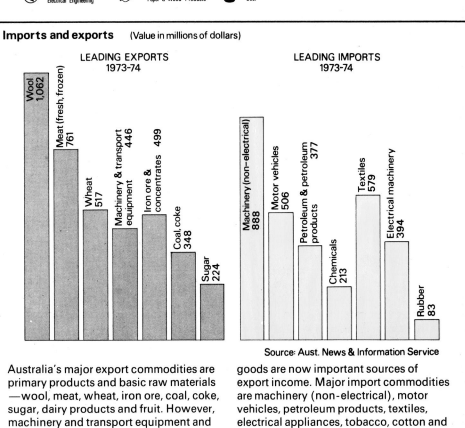

LEADING EXPORTS 1973-74

Wool 1,062
Meat (fresh, frozen) 761
Wheat 517
Machinery & transport equipment 446
Iron ore & concentrates 499
Coal, coke 348
Sugar 224

LEADING IMPORTS 1973-74

Machinery (non-electrical) 888
Motor vehicles 506
Petroleum & petroleum products 377
Chemicals 213
Textiles 579
Electrical machinery 394
Rubber 83

Source: Aust. News & Information Service

Australia's major export commodities are primary products and basic raw materials —wool, meat, wheat, iron ore, coal, coke, sugar, dairy products and fruit. However, machinery and transport equipment and an increasing range of manufactured goods are now important sources of export income. Major import commodities are machinery (non-electrical), motor vehicles, petroleum products, textiles, electrical appliances, tobacco, cotton and timber.

Gazetteer

Adelaide (34 55S 138 32E) Capital of South Australia, seaport on R. Torrens. Connection point for transcontinental railway. University, oil refining, cars, steel tubes, electrical appliances, chemicals, sugar. Pop. 868,000 (1973).

Albany (35S 118E) Western Australia. Port on King George Sound, founded in 1826 as a penal colony. Chief export fruit. Pop. 13,005 (1972).

Australian Capital Territory Seat of Federal Government and area surrounding Canberra. Highest point Mt Bimberi (1900 metres). Sheep and cattle farming. Pop. 143,843 (1972).

Ballarat (37,33S 143 15E) City in Victoria, former gold field district. Market centre, engineering, timber, bricks, tiles. Pop. 58,434 (1972).

Bendigo (36 40S 144 15E) City in Victoria. Former gold mining town. Food processing and trade, varied industries. Pop. 45,860 (1972).

Brisbane (27 25S 152 54E) Capital of Queensland and Australia's biggest river port. Exports agricultural produce; processing and agricultural-based industries, oil refining. Fine streets and parks, university, airport. Pop. 911,000 (1973).

Broken Hill (31 58S 141 29E) New South Wales. Major mining and industrial town. Silver, lead and zinc mines. Pop. 29,743 (1972).

Bunbury (33 20S 115 35E) Western Australia. Seaport and commercial centre of large pastoral, fruit-growing and timber district. New bauxite refinery for Hotham River deposits. Pop. 17,762 (1972).

Burnie (41S 146E) Tasmanian seaport. Manufactured goods, paper, pulp, chemicals, oil terminal. Pop. 20,088 (1972).

Cairns (16 55S 145 51E) Queensland. Seaport on Trinity Bay, bulk sugar port, tourist centre. Pop. 32,570 (1972).

Canberra (35 15S 149E) Capital of Australia, in Great Dividing Range. Planned city founded 1911. Seat of government, diplomatic and administrative centre, university. Pop. 185,000 (1973).

Darwin (12 20S 130 50E) Capital of Northern Territory, serving Frances Creek iron ore mines and Gove Peninsula mines. Airport, tourism, devastated by cyclone in 1974, to be rebuilt. Pop. 35,281 (1972).

Geelong (38S 144 20E) Victoria. Seaport exporting flour, meat, wool. Cars, carpets, agricultural machinery. Oil refining. Pop. 126,500 (1973).

Geraldton (28 48S 114 32E) Western Australia. Seaport, outlet for wheat belt, also exports wool and manganese, superphosphate. Pop. 15,330 (1972).

Goulborn (32 22S 149 31E) New South Wales. City commanding route across Great Dividing Range. Centre of agricultural district. Wool, shoes. Pop. 21,810 (1972).

Great Barrier Reef (From 10S–24S) Coral reef barrier off north east coast, 1600 kms. long, 160 kms. from coast, dotted with coral islands, in danger of being eaten away by starfish.

Great Dividing Range

Mountain system near east coast. Extends, under different names, from Queensland to Victoria and separates the east coast plain from the interior. Maximum altitudes in Australian Alps.

Hobart (42 50S 147 21E) Tasmania. Capital and chief port, on River Derwent. Fruit exports, zinc, cadmium, superphosphates, pulp, paper and timber, textiles. Pop. 133,080 (1973).

Kalgoorlie (30 40S 121 22E) Western Australia. Mining town on transcontinental railway. Semi-desert conditions, nickel, gold-mining. Pop. 20,784 (1972).

Kosciusko, Mount (36 27S 148 16E) In Australian Alps, New South Wales. At 2225 metres, is the highest peak in Australia. Discovered by Polish minerologist and named after Polish patriot.

Launceston (41 24S 147 8E) Tasmania. Second town of Tasmania. Wool, textiles, cars. Pop. 62,730 (1973).

Lismore (28 44S 153 21E) New South Wales. Port on Richmond River. Dairying, sugar refining, maize, potatoes, textiles, engineering. Pop. 21,300 (1973).

Melbourne (37 40S 145E) Capital of Victoria, seaport at mouth of Yarra River. Commercial centre of large region, international airport, main financial and commercial centre of Australia. Pop. 2,583,900 (1973).

Mildura (34 8S 14 27E) Victoria. Town on River Murray in major centre for irrigation area. Fruit canning, food processing, citrus and other stoned fruits. Pop. 13,190 (1972).

Mount Isa (20 42S 139 26E) Queensland. Town in Selwyn Range, important copper mining centre. Pop. 25,240 (1972).

Newcastle (32 52S 151 49E) New South Wales. Seaport at mouth of River Hunter, second city of State, leading industrial centre. Exports agricultural produce and wine from Hunter Valley. Steel, engineering, shipbuilding, chemicals. Pop. 357,770 (1973).

New South Wales State in south-east Australia. Much wealth in tablelands and mountains with equable climate well suited to arable and pastoral agriculture. Leading agricultural state in Australia, with major irrigation schemes. Coal mining and heavy industry at Newcastle, hydroelectric power from Snowy Mountains scheme. Capital Sydney. Pop. 4,754,400 (1974).

Northern Territory North Australian State. Variable rainfall, decreasing inland. Large semi-nomadic Aboriginal population. Livestock production and mining. Chief centres Darwin (capital) on north coast and Alice Springs in south. Pop. 101,700 (1974).

Perth (31 57S 115 52E) Capital of Western Australia. Serves large agricultural hinterland, many industries based on agricultural products. Well-planned, modern city, founded as gold rush town. Pop. 739,200 (1973).

Port Hedland (20 25S 118 35E) Western Australia. Seaport, with new town being built 8 kms. inland to absorb impact of Mount Newman iron ore project. Exports iron ore to Japan. Pop. 7,172 (1972).

Queensland State in north-east Australia. Rises from east coast plain to Great Dividing Range. Sub-tropical and tropical climate, population concentrated on east coast. Produces sugar cane, pineapples, bananas, cotton, sheep and beef on inland grasslands. Copper mining, lead, zinc, oil at Moonie. Great Barrier Reef along coast. Capital Brisbane. Pop. 1,968,600 (1974).

Rockhampton (23 22S 150 32E) Queensland. Port on River Fitzroy, commercial capital of central Queensland. Fruit canning, meat preserving, cotton-ginning, railway works. Pop. 48,188 (1972).

South Australia The "desert state". Physical features include mountains in south east, Lake Eyre basin (12 metres below sea level), the Nullarbor Plain in the south-west. Sheep in the south-east. Intensive agriculture in Murray River valley. The state capital, Adelaide, has most of the industry and 60% of the population. Pop. 1,216,000 (1974).

Sydney (33 53S 151 10E) Capital of New South Wales. Oldest and largest city of Australia, with superb harbour, large population. Magnificent bridge and opera house, university, cathedrals, international airport, botanical gardens. Oil refining, wool trade, consumer goods. Pop. 2,874,380 (1973).

Tasmania Island state. Plateau with fertile valleys, temperate climate, forest and grasslands. Grain, fruit, cattle, aluminium, copper, zinc, lead, tin, silver. Hydroelectric power from Gordon River scheme. Capital Hobart. Pop. 399,500 (1974).

Toowoomba (27 32S 151 56E) Queensland. Railway centre and market town for wheat and dairy produce. Food processing, iron foundry using local coal. Pop. 61,000 (1974).

Victoria State traversed by Great Dividing Range. Temperate climate, smallest and most densely populated mainland state. Major industrial area, wool, grain, dairy produce, fruit, gold, tin, natural gas off east coast. Capital Melbourne. Pop. 3,626,800 (1974).

Western Australia Largest state, comprising nearly one third of continent but only 8% of population. Capital Perth in fertile area similar to Mediterranean. Hamersley and Kimberley Ranges, Gibson Desert in interior. Rich mineral deposits, intensive agriculture in south-west, wheat and sheep in interior. Pop. 1,091,100 (1974).

Wollongong (34 25S 150 54E) New South Wales. Coal mining city, iron and steel works, fertilizers, chemicals, bricks. Also includes Port Kembla, a major industrial area and shipbuilding centre. Pop. 205,780 (1973).

Index

AUSTRALIA Political

	International Boundaries			State Boundaries
⬛ ⊙ ◎ ○ ∘	Cities and Towns			Railways
	Seasonal Lakes			Main Roads
			✈	Airports

Scale 1:20,000,000

0   200   400 kilometres
0   100   200   300   400 miles

Projection : Bonne

Place labels

INDONESIA

Jogjakarta
Sorakarta
Semarang
Surabaja
Malang

Sumba
Sumbawa
Flores
Timor

IRIAN

PAPUA NEW GUINEA
PORT MORESBY
Daru
Meruake
Samarai
Weipa

INDIAN OCEAN

Timor Sea

Coral Sea

PACIFIC OCEAN

Tasman Sea

SOUTHERN OCEAN

Tropic of Capricorn

Northern Territory
Darwin
Rum Jungle
Pine Creek
Katherine
Larrimah
Daly Waters
Tennant Creek
Alice Springs
Camooweal

Western Australia
Wyndham
Hall's Creek
Derby
Broome
Port Hedland
Roebourne
Onslow
Marble Bar
Mount Goldsworthy
Peak Hill
Mount Magnet
Carnarvon
Learmonth
Geraldton
Northam
Bonnie Rock
Narrogin
Leonora
Kalgoorlie
Boulder
Norseman
Esperance
Perth
Fremantle
Bunbury
Augusta
Albany

Queensland
Cooktown
Cairns
Laura
Normanton
Croydon
Forsayth
Georgetown
Charters Towers
Townsville
Bowen
Mackay
Rockhampton
Gladstone
Mt. Morgan
Bundaberg
Maryborough
Gympie
Kajabbi
Cloncurry
Mount Isa
Dajarra
Winton
Hughenden
Longreach
Emerald
Yaraka
Charleville
Quilpie
Cunnamulla
Roma
Dalby
Toowoomba
Warwick
Brisbane
Ipswich
Dirranbandi

South Australia
Oodnadatta
Woomera
Oodea
Penong
Deakin
Eucla
Evre
Kingston
Port Augusta
Port Pirie
Wallaroo
Port Lincoln
Adelaide
L. Eyre
L. Torrens

New South Wales
Bourke
Nyngan
Cobar
Broken Hill
Bombala
Dubbo
Bathurst
Cunnamulla
Moree
Tamworth
Armidale
Lismore
Grafton
Maitland
Newcastle
Lithgow
Parramatta
Sydney
Wollongong
Wagga Wagga
Hay
Albury
Kingaroy

Australian Capital Territory
CANBERRA
AUST. CAPITAL TERR.

Victoria
Mildura
Ballarat
Bendigo
Geelong
Melbourne
Maryborough
Portland
Warrnambool
Goulburn
Traralgon
Yarram
Bairnsdale

Tasmania
Devonport
Launceston
Queenstown
Hobart

Rivers
Diamantina
Darling
Murray
Murrumbidgee
L. Mackay
L. Disappointment

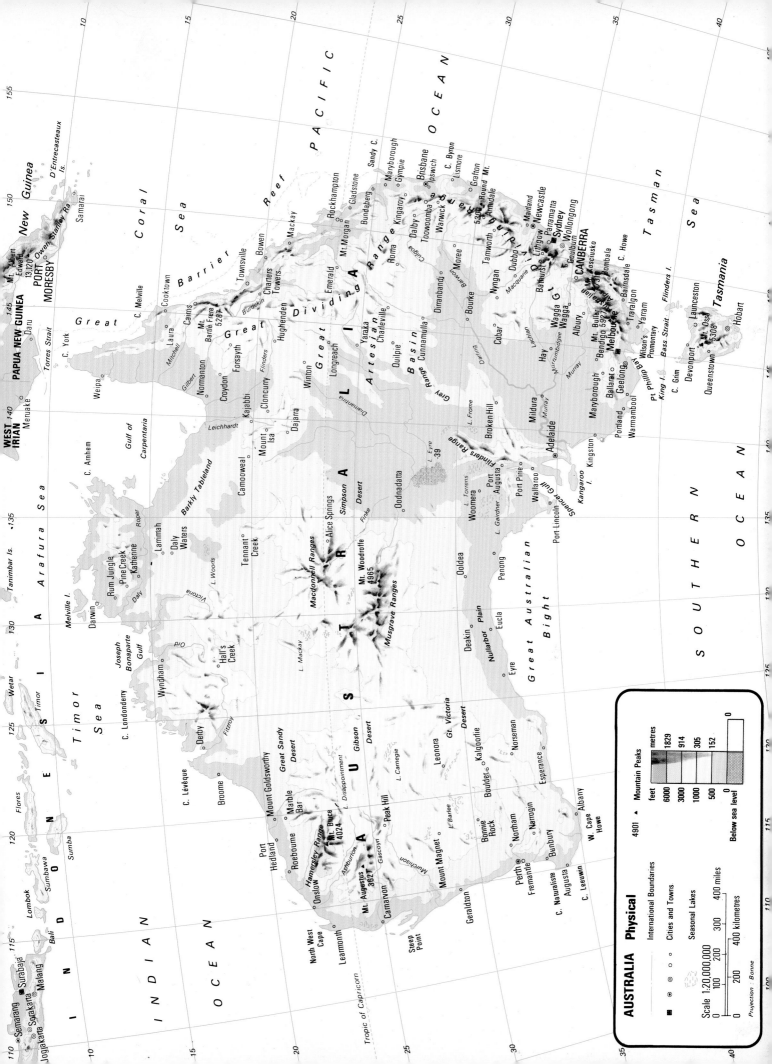

AUSTRALIA Physical

	International Boundaries
▪ ◉ ⊙ ◦	Cities and Towns
	Seasonal Lakes

▲ 4901 Mountain Peaks

metres	feet
1829	6000
914	3000
305	1000
152	500
0	0
Below sea level	

Scale 1:20,000,000

0 100 200 300 400 miles
0 100 200 300 400 kilometres

Projection : Bonne